From Ash to Fire

P9-BZG-961

From Ash to Fire

A Contemporary Journey through the
Interior Castle
of
Teresa of Avila

Carolyn Humphreys

New City Press

Published in the United States by New City Press
202 Cardinal Rd., Hyde Park, NY 12538
©1992 New City Press, New York

Library of Congress Cataloging-in-Publication Data:

Humphreys, Carolyn.
    From ash to fire : a contemporary journey
  through the Interior Castle of Teresa of Avila / Carolyn Humphreys.

    Includes bibliographical references.
    ISBN 1-56548-040-6 : $9.95
    1. Teresa, of Avila, Saint, 1515-1582. Moradas. 2. Spiritual
  life—Catholic Church.   I. Teresa, of Avila, Saint, 1515-1582.
  Moradas. II. Title.
  BX2179.T4M7245   1992
  248.4'82—dc20   92-14861

1st printing: September 1992
4th printing: August 1997

Printed in Canada

CONTENTS

FOREWORD

It gives me great pleasure to write a Foreword to this book, subtitled *A Contemporary Journey through the Interior Castle*. Authors generally agree that the *Interior Castle* is Teresa's most orderly and mature work on our prayer journey to God, a timeless classic in the spiritual field. This modern commentary is a testimony to its abiding value and its relevance to our day.

The author writes in a very attractive and incisive style—reaching even to literary eloquence, at times, as in the Prelude which resounds with musical tonalities. She shows a sound psychological approach in her commentary. It is full of solid insight, keen intuition and wise counsels for the spiritual journey; always insisting on the integration of the human person. Prayer is not an isolated activity, but must be part of the very warp and woof of daily life.

In this commentary, the path and progress of prayer are illustrated invariably with reference to our contemporary life and modern situations. So it should appeal to a modern reader, while following the classic seven stages of Teresa's mansions.

It is significant that this volume comes from the pen of a Secular Carmelite in California. One of the great spiritual manifestations of our day is the desire for a prayer-filled life, flourishing in the context of a materialistic society. For Carmelites, desiring to be in the forefront of prayer movements in the Church, it is very gratifying that the Secular Carmelite movement is growing in numbers and influence.

This movement, which represents a flowering of the Carmelite charisma among the laity, is surely one of the significant aspects of the Church today. Through its membership, its congresses and its life style, it is having a considerable impact on Church life, particularly in the United States. It is drawing many people close to the Lord in contemplative prayer, and providing a valid testimony to prayer as the very heartbeat of the Church's life.

I pray that this book, which is so obviously the fruit of personal reflection, will guide many prayerful people through the *Moradas* to the very center of their souls which is also the crystal dwelling place of our Lord and Savior.

Michael Buckley, O.C.D., Provincial
Discalced Carmelites, Western Province

ACKNOWLEDGEMENTS

There are special people who have enriched my ongoing pilgrimage of life. They have played a part in the writing of this book. Fragments of their wisdom appear within these pages. They have made this particular interpretation of the *Interior Castle* possible. I sincerely wish to thank them.

A few individuals merit acknowledgement. My heartfelt and very special thank you is graciously given to: Patrick Sugrue, O.C.D., Barbara Wilson, Penny Brown, O.C.D.S., Ernest Nosari, O.C.D.S., M.S.W., Hannah Herlihy, D.M.J., Edward Leahy, O.C.D., Carmen Fojo, O.C.D.S., M.S., Tina Scott, O.T.R., Robert O'Hanlon, O.C.D.S., R.N., and Geri Aman, O.T.R.

PRELUDE

The interior castle is open to any individual who desires to live and grow in the unity of Christ and his eucharist. This journey is a growth in love which is rooted in the life of Jesus and lived in the everyday activities of one's own particular life style.

The interior castle is a journey in prayer. It is prayer as experienced by Teresa of Jesus. In this castle she takes a person from the beginning prayer of the neophyte to the transforming prayer of mystical union. Teresa's variants of prayer rise like a blending of melodies in a symphony of love to God. Each mansion in Teresa's castle represents a separate suite, and in each suite the lyrics and harmonies merge in a praise to God and a progression to the next mansion. Teresa's symphony of love holds silent music and great crescendos of joy. Her ongoing aria of prayer is never flat, but filled with consonance, dissonance, atonalities, profound chant, happy rhythms and other instrumental properties that stretch and strengthen a person's journey in love and faith.

The *Interior Castle* is a book that is revered and held dear by the Discalced Carmelites. The secular members, cloistered nuns and friars of this order seek to live the prayer of Christ with emphasis on the contemplative aspect of this prayer. Prayer is their primary apostolate. Even though most Discalced Carmelites view the *Interior Castle* as a sound guide for prayer, many do not experience the extraordinary phenomena, which Teresa describes so well, that may be a part of mystical prayer. In her master work Teresa welcomes everyone to grow in the life and love of God.

Those individuals who desire to embark on a spiritual journey are people on a pilgrimage of faith. Faith is their sustaining force. It becomes a faith that is grounded in love and geared to the supernatural. Strength comes from God as steps are made into the abyss of his infinite love. To embark on a spiritual journey is to direct one's energies to the fulfillment of personhood at its highest level. It is one that seeks to grasp the height and depth and breadth and length of the love of Christ. It takes courage and perseverance. Teresa urges her pilgrims onward: "Let nothing disturb you. Let nothing frighten you."

INTRODUCTION

During the last few decades there appears to be a renewed interest in the spiritual journey. The spiritual classics are enjoying a new readership and efforts have been made to understand them in the light of modern times. There have been workshops, seminars, and centers set up to promote unity and growth of the body, mind and spirit. There seems to be a shift from looking outward for fulfillment to turning inward for interior enlightenment. Deep-seated yearnings of the spirit within seek recognition. People desire a satisfaction that grants them a true peace of heart.

The spiritual journey is the oldest and longest journey known to humankind. It has fascinated and intrigued cultures down through the centuries. Inner spiritual experiences are found in all religious traditions around the world. With the coming of the incarnate Christ, the Christian spiritual journey was born.

This spiritual journey began its evolution during the early Christian era. Gradually the spiritual masters defined and developed various stages of spiritual growth. In the fourth century a Father of the Eastern Church, Gregory of Nyssa, pioneered the concept of progression along this journey. He was hailed as a militant spiritual thinker and developed his ideas by reading scripture from the context of spirituality present in the passages along one's life.

His major contribution was that there was progression in the spiritual life. He introduced the idea of stages and viewed the spiritual life as a continual growth process. He based this concept on Paul's theme of moving forward. "Forgetting the past, I strain ahead for what is still to come" (Phil 3:13).

The great Augustine, a Father of the Western Church, was noted for being influential in developing this theme further by giving these stages names and descriptions. The first stage was the purgative way. During this stage a person's chief concern was his or her awareness of sin, sorrow for sin, and desire to make amends because God has been offended. The second stage was the illuminative way. Its main feature was the enlightenment of a person's mind regarding the ways of God, and a clearer understanding of God's will in a person's life style. The third, and final stage, was the unitive way. Here, there was a continual awareness of being in God's presence. The individual also, in a loving way, strove to conform his or her will to the will of God.

In the sixteenth century, Teresa of Avila expanded these stages from three to seven and developed them within her book called the *Interior Castle*.

Before we plunge into the *Interior Castle*, let us consider the spiritual life and its development as it is seen today. It is important that an individual does not see spiritual development as a separate and distinct entity that is set apart from all other areas of development within one's life. The spiritual life cannot be disconnected from a person and observed as a unique form of growth. The spiritual journey is an awareness of the most important part of a totally functioning human being. This journey connects an individual with the infinite God, influences all aspects and activities of one's life, and continues beyond death. However, it cannot stand alone nor grow autonomously. As an example, let us parallel sexual development, our development as men and women, with spiritual development. If an individual's sexuality is ignored, his or her spirituality may deteriorate or become distorted. A high degree of spiritual development cannot coexist compatibly with a sexual development that is fixated in any pre-adult stage. A person cannot be spiritually viable if he or she is situated in a state of asexual aloofness which serves as a protective shield from the give and take of life. A preoccupation with one's sexuality can also interfere with or impede an individual's spiritual growth. The key word here is integration. A person is not composed of separate developmental patterns of growth, where each pattern has its own independent rate of growth and develops in an isolated fashion apart from other developmental areas. This can be illustrated in greater detail by observing the growth and integration that takes place in one area of development known as physical development.

Physical development depends on the growth and interaction of various systems in the body. A system is an organized grouping of related structures or organs that perform certain functions. There are nine major systems within the body. The skeletal system supports the body. The muscular system gives the body countless expressions of movement. The nervous system controls, coordinates and integrates a myriad of activities that goes on inside the body. It is the organizer and communicator of all the systems. The endocrine system regulates hormones which are the main regulators of metabolism, growth, development, reproduction, and responses to stress. The circulatory system's primary function is transportation. The respiratory system makes it possible for blood to exchange carbon dioxide for oxygen. It is the lifeline of the body. The digestive system prepares food for absorption and use by the millions of body cells and rids the body of the wastes of digestion. The urinary system produces urine and eliminates it from the body, and the reproductive system generates new life. Each system is dependent on the other systems for functioning. What would bones be without muscles? Inert. What would the digestive organs be without the urinary tract? Poisoned. What would the circulatory system be without oxygen? Asphyxiated. Where would any of us be without the endocrine and reproductive systems? Not in existence.

We can see, then, that each system cannot stand alone. So it is with the various developmental areas. A person's cognitive, physical, psychological, emotional, social, sexual, and spiritual development may be considered separately for the sake of academic knowledge, but as they exist within a living person they must be considered together. There needs to be a harmonic blending of body, mind and spirit. Dysfunction occurs if there is an acceleration of, delay in, or denial of one or more developmental areas. A human person is a holistic being striving for full potential. Holism tells us that human persons have a reality and existence that is greater than the sum of their parts. However, the desire to go beyond oneself cannot be established if great distances exist among the maturation levels of one's developmental stages. Since the spiritual journey is beyond self, an integration and unity of all developmental areas is needed in order to maintain wholesome attitudes within. All dimensions of a person are motivated in one way or another during an individual's spiritual journey. No matter how dedicated one is to the pursuit of the spiritual, this area cannot mature alone.

The spiritual journey is a slow process. It cannot be rushed. One cannot purchase a ticket for a quick tour of the interior castle. The spiritual journey will require a distancing from cultural and personal attitudes that dictate values, principles, and how a person is to spend his or her time and energies if these attitudes go against God's love. The spiritual journey is not a source for health, wealth, wisdom, psychological comfort or social esteem. It is not a security blanket that will provide all the answers or protect one from the problems of life. When an individual is embarking on a spiritual venture it cannot be a total time consumer, ultimate energy concern, or do or die endeavor. Space is also needed for routine daily activities, work, rest, relaxing hobbies, personal interests and other components that create a well-balanced day. To channel all efforts into a pursuit of the spiritual would only lead to a lopsided life style that ends in fanaticism.

The spiritual journey within the interior castle is rich and profound. The spiritual vision that the castle reflects is rooted in the beauty of the tradition of Carmel. In order to understand the depths and breadth of this beauty, let us briefly examine some of the attributes of the Carmelite charism.

Prayer is the focal point of Carmel. This prayer is without frills. It is the simple prayer of Jesus when he got up early in the morning and went out to a place of solitude to pray. It is the prayer one dwells upon when one goes into a room and shuts the door and prays to God in secret. It is a prayer from the heart in which a person enters into his or her own center and flows through it to unite with the center of God who abides deeply within. When a person is serious about prayer, there will be no excuses because he or she cannot find the time to pray. Prayer is never a duty or an obligation. It is the way in which an individual builds a loving relationship with God.

For the Carmelite, contemplative prayer is at the heart of everything. Contemplation is neither alien nor macabre. It has nothing to do with ethereal beings that have perpetual, celestial expressions on their faces, fluffy angels, lasting levitations, supersonic spirits, or any other strange phenomena that is conjured up in the mind.

Contemplation is not as strange as it sounds. In the secular sense, contemplation occurs when thoughts become insights. There is no awareness of the passage of time, nor is there an awareness of one's present environment. When a person views or considers anything with great attention, there is contemplation. This is evident when viewing a great work of art, or looking at the majesty of a natural wonder such as the Grand Canyon, Yosemite, or the Sequoia Redwoods. It may also occur at a concert or ballet. In the secular context, contemplation considers the event from the perspective of the event alone, or from the perspective of the human element that was involved in creating the event.

Spiritual contemplation completes secular contemplation. Contemplation, in the spiritual sense, is the pondering of a person, place or thing, which then directs one's heart and mind to God. Contemplation is being aware of the divine presence in everything. This is characterized by going beyond labels, living in the here and now, and doing tasks for themselves rather than doing them as a means to get to another task. To illustrate this, let us consider the activity involved in mailing a letter. When we go beyond labels, we liberate ourselves from categorizing any person, place or thing we may encounter when walking to the mailbox. There is no stereotyping, only a delight in experiencing the creative gifts of God. If we are walking in the here and now, we do not reflect upon the events of yesterday nor the problems of tomorrow. We are experiencing the joy of the present moment. If we are doing the task for itself, we are not concerned about what has been written or getting the letter in the mailbox as quickly as possible so it can be picked up by the mail carrier. Instead, we are filled with wonder at the way our bodies move when walking. The change in pressure on the soles of our feet as the ground changes from sloping lawns to crunching leaves to hard pavement gives us a greater sensation of balance. The quiet rhythm of our footfalls sound a gentle cadence. A light, cool breeze may feel more refreshing on our faces. Tasks done in the present reality should be vehicles for an increase in faith, hope and love. Contemplation travels below the surface of the familiar and finds an appreciation in the hidden treasures that occur in daily life. We grow in contemplation as we grow in our receptivity to everything. Contemplation is a way of loving and a way of being that transcends the obvious value of things. Moments of contemplative prayer are usually unexpected and experienced at different levels. These gifted moments give depth to a normal, routine activity or reflection. We become enthralled and lost in the graced light of the moment. Everything is embraced as one with the One. This is matched with an interior unity. Contemplative prayer is a simple, enjoyable, intuitive, deep resting in the beauty of God which is present in all his creation. The Carmelite is most at home when he or she is cultivating the art of contemplative prayer. Spiritual contemplation finds personal wholeness within the mysterious wholesomeness of God.

Silence is another important charism of Carmel. "Be still and know that I am God," the psalmist sings. "Your strength will be in silence and in hope." Sound prayer begins in silence. Inner quiet brings an attentiveness to God. Silence here does not mean the mere absence of sound nor a physical stillness. Both are helpful and necessary, but the gem of silence lies in a quietness of the heart and mind. This allows for a deep communing with God. A quiet mind means letting go of desires, goals, plans, words, concepts, clatter, worries, work to be done, and other busy things that clutter the mind in prayer. All these elements close communication between oneself and God. A quiet mind at prayer flows into a silent heart which overflows into one's words and actions outside of prayer. Silence during prayer is a very natural way of prayer for the Carmelite. Solitude walks hand in hand with silence. Solitude is genuine if an individual withdraws from people in order to be closely united to God in prayer. Solitude is not escapism, nor is it isolationism. Solitude is experienced as an opportunity. It is a time to be alone with God alone. It is a space to discover the vastness of the spiritual. It is a place where prayerful contemplation is allowed to develop and grow.

Teresa expects anyone who desires to understand and live the Carmelite charism to be daring in love, willing to take risks and not be afraid of looking foolish. These expectations come from the roots of Carmel which are deeply embedded in the Old Testament. Carmel's prophetic spirit centers around Elijah. Like this prophet, the life, actions, and words of the Carmelite are as signs of God to all humankind. Like Elijah, the Carmelite's life is a continual search for God, and this is an ongoing challenge to the whole person.

Mary walks with the Carmelite as he or she searches for God. It is she who leads a person deeper and deeper into the mystery of Christ. Mary lived in mystery. She lived God's will without fully understanding it. She lived by faith. Her life was an all consuming act of love. In union with Mary, the Carmelite lives and sings her song at eventide as a canticle of praise to God.

The Carmelite's life is as a great river flowing to God. The Carmelite may be seen on the surface of this river where all activities take place. There are the tug boats of work, the garbage barges of cleanup tasks, the motor boats of ministry, the row boats of recreation, the steam boats of maintenance duties, and the rafts of rest and relaxation. However, the Carmelite dwells, essentially, at the bottom of the river. Here, at its quiet depths, God exists in faith, love and trust. Here is where the Carmelite comes after activities on the surface of the river are done. There is a simple and gentle repose in God here where one can resubmerge into the true meaning and mystery of life.

So it can be seen that Carmelite spirituality is not a rapid journey from point A to a distant point B via a mystical arrow. It is not a transcendence out of oneself into an ultimate cosmic reality. It is not a rigid, systematized, tedious, slow progression of events that leads a person to the center of the supreme consciousness. Carmelite spirituality is based on and flows from an intimate union with the indwelling God. The goal of the spiritual life, for the Carmelite, is union with God through love and prayer. The Carmelite's emphasis on God's presence is his presence within. The God in one's core of being. The indwelling Trinity in one's deepest center. The Carmelite's spiritual life is a strong and viable interior life. It is a loving and prayerful experience of God at one's innermost still point.

Roots of the vine

The author of the *Interior Castle* is Teresa de Cepeda y Ahumada. She is also known as Teresa de Jesus, or Saint Teresa of Avila. Who was this woman? What was she like? Her daughters, the Carmelite nuns of Terre Haute, Indiana, share with us this brief, but poignant, account of her life.

"Teresa of Avila, a Spanish Carmelite nun of the sixteenth century brought to the Church a new lived expression of the ancient rule of Our Lady of Mount Carmel. Living in Spain, after the Council of Trent, in times very much like our own, she determined to restore the primitive rule of Carmel which had been relaxed and to infuse into it a deeper spirit of service to the Church through prayer. To accomplish this, she founded her first monastery of Saint Joseph in Avila, in 1562. The new community was a small group of cloistered nuns, dedicated to a life of prayer in solitude, to poverty, and to an intense sisterly charity. During her lifetime, Teresa founded seventeen monasteries of nuns, and, with John of the Cross as her associate, she restored the primitive rule in newly established houses of the Spanish Carmelite friars. Before she died in 1582, she had the consolation of seeing her foundations of nuns and friars established as a separate province of the Carmelite Order, having its own distinct spirit, laws, and government.

"Characteristic of Teresa were her vivacity and charm, her determination, and her dauntless courage to carry out anything and everything God asked of her. She possessed eminent common sense, with a warm human personality that was enriched with great intelligence, and God given experience of the highest ways of prayer. Her writings display the variety of both her human and supernatural gifts and, at the same time, provide authentic and lofty teachings about prayer and the spiritual life, unequalled in Christian literature. In 1970 Pope Paul VI declared her a Doctor of the Church, signifying the validity and universality of her doctrine.

"Teresa is an example and guide for men and women of this century in every situation and life style. All those who love life, whose hearts are filled with noble ambitions, who are called to great exploits or to the heroicity of daily duty, might well take her as their patroness. This saint, aflame with love of God and alive with friendship for all her associates, shows us that holiness and wholesomeness are inseparable companions of sublime sanctity. In action and in prayer she challenges us to follow her to the heights.

"Prayer was for Teresa of Avila an intimate and solitary conversation with our best friend, Jesus. She teaches us that there is no better road to God than the road of prayer; and she urges everyone to set out on this road with determination. Living in a time of upheaval, she warns us to believe only those persons who have patterned their lives on Christ. All her life, her prayers and her activities were directed to the upbuilding of the Church. Her last words are an echo of all Teresa of Avila believed and lived, and a beacon of truth for us. 'I am so happy,' she said, 'to die a daughter of the Church.' "

Teresa was a woman of multifaced charisms. She realized the value of intimate friendships. This particular charism set her apart, as did many of her special gifts, from the spirituality that was popular during her time. Teresa had a special ability to foster and maintain deep and lasting relationships. Her friends were an enriching source of support and comfort throughout her life.

One highly treasured friend of Teresa's was Jerome Gracian. This Carmelite friar was especially loved by Teresa. His very presence could bring laughter to her heart even though she was concerned with many things. Father Gracian followed Teresa in the reform, and became the first provincial of the newly established Province of Discalced Carmelite Friars.

It was through a conversation between Teresa and Jerome, at the Carmel of Toledo, that the idea of writing more about the spiritual journey to God arose. Teresa had already written two books. *The Way of Perfection* was a practical book of advice and counsel designed to accompany and explain her primitive constitutions. The *Life* was referred to as "The book of the mercies of God." It was an autobiographical account of Teresa's spiritual life.

When Jerome Gracian was provincial, he visited Teresa at her convent in Toledo. They spoke of many things concerning her spiritual life. Teresa expressed a desire to elaborate on a certain spiritual point that she touched upon in her *Life*. She regretted that she could not do this since the manuscript was being held in the archives of the scrupulous Spanish Inquisition. Teresa had a respectful fear of the Inquisition. Gracian realized the dangers that could come from a more detailed personal account of her spiritual journey. Since the *Life* could not be returned for additions or revisions, Gracian told Teresa to recall what she could, think of other matters, and write another book. He advised her to put her doctrine and other information down in a general way without mentioning herself as the person from whom these thoughts came.

As much as she loved Jerome, Teresa balked at his idea to write another book. She was sixty-two at this time. She felt she was too old. She tried to beg off by stating that she had to attend to many business matters. She did not have the time. She only desired to continue with her spinning and live the quiet life with her sisters. She called herself a stupid woman and asserted that many, many books were already written on prayer by learned theologians. She had a poor memory. Her health could not take the strain. She had been given many difficult things to do in the past under obedience, but her present task of writing about prayer seemed the most difficult of all.

Teresa had many repugnant feelings about this task, but her dedication to obedience helped her along. Teresa firmly believed that by completing this task through obedience the impossibility of it would become less difficult. Her prayer upon beginning the book was: "May he, in whose mercy I trust, and who has helped me in other, more difficult things, so as to favor me, do this work for me." She began the book with aversion. When she finished, she had to admit that the work brought her much happiness and she considered her labor to be well spent.

There are several concepts one should be aware of when undertaking a prayerful study of the *Interior Castle*. The title alone tells us that Teresa's writing style is allegorical. She used symbolic representations to describe actions or truths about human existence. She desired to share her insights about the beauty of a person in a state of grace. She gave much thought to the subject she would use to illustrate this. She saw a person who was grace filled as a beautiful palace of priceless worth. Later, this idea merged into a beautiful crystal castle with seven mansions. The seventh mansion was at the center where the King of Glory resided in splendor illuminating everything with his light. Outside of the castle, everything was foul and dark and infested with toads and snakes and other venomous creatures. The darkness represented serious sin. The light represented grace. This was the image that Teresa wished everyone might see. It seemed to her that no one would enter the dark, hideous world of sin when they were aware of the bright beauty and splendor of God's life and love which is grace.

Teresa's allegories fill her other works. Her allegories have a delightful quality and are very necessary because, when describing extraordinary events, an individual must relate the unknown with the known within his or her own cultural and historical setting. Teresa first described a grace filled person as a palace of gold and precious jewels in *The Way of Perfection*. Jesus tells us that in heaven there are many mansions. Teresa likens the spirit of a person in a state of grace to a diamond or very clear crystal globe in which there are also many rooms. Today, if a person were writing about the spiritual journey, or union with God through prayer, he or she might choose an entirely different subject. If one were thinking of a descriptive theme for Teresa's journey at the present time, one might consider calling it the "interior universe." The solar system would be a point of reference. The sun would represent God, and our astronaut pilgrim would travel from planet to planet, beginning at the outermost Pluto and navigating toward Venus, and then on to the sun. This would be an extensive journey in inner space since each heavenly body has its own star clusters, moons, and orbit to explore.

One last comment about Teresa's writing style. The *Interior Castle* is her most organized work. Now, those people who are familiar with Teresa must be smiling at this point because it is well known that organization is not listed among her writing qualities. This sentence may be rephrased to read: the *Interior Castle* is her most organized work when it is compared with her other books. When people read Teresa, they soon find that her presentations do not follow an orderly and logical progression. This is not her style. She digresses, regresses, progresses and vacillates from side to side quite often. Her style may resemble a gambler looking at a stack of poker chips that have been knocked down. There are edges of circles over and under edges of other circles. At the end our gambler knows where he or she stands when all the chips have been collected. Teresa's order in the *Interior Castle* can be viewed at best as a disorderly order which, in the end, makes very good sense.

Teresa began writing the *Interior Castle* on the eve of the Feast of the Trinity in June of 1577. She finished it in November of that same year. In the interim, for a period of three months, she was involved in the work of the order which gave her no time for writing activities.

It took her only three months to complete this book, yet, Teresa considered it her masterpiece, her best work. It was also her most spiritual work. Another title used for the *Interior Castle* was *The Mansions*. However, Teresa did not want those who read her book to envision a castle or a mansion as she knew them or as they are known today. Her castle was not to be the medieval fortress guarded by high walls and gallant knights which protected kings and queens and maidens fair and had prototypes of Robin Hood and his merry men scurrying about the forest. Neither were Teresa's mansions to be stately, majestic, impressive buildings with wide corridors that led to specific places, and aristocratic halls which housed precious artifacts. Teresa did not even want her castle to hold a renowned seat of magic and mysterious legends as the rustic Castle of Blarney holds in venerable Old Ireland.

Teresa saw her castle as a circular edifice. Within each circle there were many rooms. If we were to look at the castle from the top, it would resemble concentric circles patterned like a target with the bull's eye at the center. The bull's eye is followed by a series of circles each larger than the one inside of it. The outermost circle would be the first mansion and in this mansion would be many rooms. It would contain more rooms than any other mansion since it is located on the outer edge. This could be compared to a jigsaw puzzle because the external border of the puzzle contains the most numerous pieces of the puzzle. As the mansion circles decrease in size, going ever inward, so does the number of rooms within each mansion until there is only one room in the seventh mansion where God dwells in eternal splendor.

Teresa's castle as seen from a side view can resemble an artichoke or an onion. Here we can see that the journey toward the center not only involves movements that are forward and backward and side to side, but also involves ascents and descents within each circle. If we use the artichoke for an example, we can see how each of the leaves must be peeled off before the tender, tasty heart of the artichoke is exposed. In the onion, we observe that removal of the parchment-like skin, layer after layer, can bring us to the succulent core. Every skin can represent parts of ourselves that grate against God's redeeming love. The "pearl" inside the core shows that the interior dwelling of God is deeply located. Through the miracle of grace we can see his light and love flow through the layers of self. His light transforms so that we become more aware of his strong light at our deepest center.

When one embarks on a journey there are always a few wise guidelines to take along the way. So it is with the interior castle's spiritual path. There are no short cuts in an individual's growth as a spiritual being. The journey through the mansions can be likened to the slow emergence of an awakened person from the darkness of sin to the lightness of God's loving power.

During our journey through the interior castle, there will be occasions in which the term "world" will be used. This term has two distinct meanings. In the context of the castle pilgrimage, this word will not be associated with God's creation. "World" will be used for anything that estranges one from God, or anything that opposes his goodness. It designates a place where people live without faith. The spiritual reality is suppressed by a zest for consumerism and opulence. Anything concerning God is nonsense and the elements of this environment continue to crucify Christ. This self-serving world is one of political propaganda, nuclear warheads, human idolatry and slick operators. Economic pride runs neck and neck with social pride and intellectual pride. The clenched fist confronts hate with hate, violence with violence and evil with evil. This world is populated with a society that thrives on quick action, fast relief, immediate answers and instant pleasures. Disrespect is shown toward persons, places and things. Its beatitude of life is: Blessed is the man who thinks about himself first.

Because each mansion of the interior castle has many rooms to explore, a person who is investigating a room may find that it leads to another room, then another room and yet another room inside the same mansion. An individual may find that he or she can remain in a particular mansion for a long, long time. Not to worry! When a person looks at a mountain range, how many peaks does it have? When a person climbs a specific mountain within the range, does he or she find more peaks? Of course! Explore! When one is on a specific mountain one travels up and down various peaks. That is okay. In Teresa's castle there is no rush to get out of one mansion and into another. No neat little trail guide is available which states this is what to do next. There is no need to hurry. An individual is not compelled, nor should he or she feel a need, to hasten to the throne room. Feel free to remain for a long time in a single mansion. Roam around its different rooms! There are no categorized stages of prayer. One progresses forward, one slips back, one wavers from side to side. No problem! God leads people by different ways. Do not restrict the movements of the Holy Spirit. Feel free to roam with liberty under God's graces. The road of the interior life is usually obscure. It is not readily understandable. The spiritual life that goes on inside the castle is a complex matter involving each individual's unique capacities. It involves a diversity of ways and a differing of spiritual depths. The seven mansions represent loosely-knit stages and allow for a wide range of variations in each stage.

The seven mansions of the interior castle are separated into two groups. The first group is composed of the first three mansions. This is where, in a general way, God intervenes in a person's prayer life. Active prayer is achieved. It is practiced through human efforts and the ordinary help of grace. The person cooperates with grace. These mansions can be related to asceticism in the sense that the individual is "given to exercises"—which is the literal translation of asceticism from the Greek. These exercises bring an individual closer to God. Through God's inspiration and one's own efforts, one offers to God various things that one feels would be pleasing to him. Teresa did not spend much time writing about these stages because she felt that they were more than adequately explained in spiritual books already written.

The second group contains mansions four through seven. These mansions dwell on the increased activity of the Holy Spirit within a person. The intellectual work in prayer is slowly being changed to spiritual intuition. These mansions deal with the mystical elements of the spiritual life. Here Teresa discusses the forms and degrees of mystical prayer and the experiences that can happen during them.

It will come as no surprise to know that the gate of entry to the interior castle is prayer. Prayer is the door that opens a human being up to the mystery of God. It sets into motion a personal relationship with God who is present in the very depths of one's being. Prayer is an expression of who a Christian is. Without prayer there is no life in the castle. When an individual lives in a spirit of prayer, life flows from the indwelling God. Fidelity to the word or wordless beauty of daily orisons nurtures this prayerful presence. Prayer not only gets one into the interior castle, but also is the cause of one's progression through it. Prayer is a person's response to grace and the inner call of God. Movement along a journey in faith flows through the delicate actions within prayer and the gentle workings of grace. Prayer gradually takes an individual from the external, egocentric self to the internal, Christocentric self. When Teresa speaks of the interior life, the spiritual life, she is speaking of prayer. Prayer is the key in a person's quest for God.

With these directives in mind, let us now begin our journey into the interior castle.

First Mansion

AT THE OUTER EDGE OF THE CASTLE

Teresa gives us a lovely prologue before she describes, in detail, the interior of the first mansion and the people who dwell there. She presents to us a similarity between a human being in a state of grace and the quality of the mansions near the center of her castle. This comparison is only to be considered equal in splendor when the center of her castle is matched with a person who is filled with the life and love of God. The heart of the person then resembles a resplendent elegance which is equal to the beauty of the higher mansions. A heart so God filled, is a place of blissful joy and unfathomed delight. Jesus takes great pleasure in this type of individual. He finds great contentment in a grace filled person because that person is a true reflection of his Father's image and likeness. The beauty of God's creation is authentically manifested in a person who is sincerely striving to do God's will. Because this beauty is so sublime, it is impossible to understand with the human intellect. The glorious grandeur and elegance that radiates from a heart filled with God's life and love blossoms forth in such a way that transcends mere human cognitive powers.

To be aware of the interior beauty of God's grace is to be aware of one's true self and one's relationship to God. The greater this awareness, the greater a human being is fused into God. The lesser the awareness, the greater a human being is fused into self. It would be quite foolish to limit one's concerns to one's physical self and external ornaments. Through faith, an individual knows there is an internal spirit that requires tender, loving care. It comes as no surprise that the beauty of the spirit fades when care and attention are not given to it. If a person has a lovely spring garden with many brightly colored flowers blossoming and blooming about, what happens when they are not watered and cared for? They all dry up and become ugly. The spirit within may also fail to thrive if a person is completely dedicated to the primping and pampering of his or her face, hair, skin, nails and physique. A continual involvement in these activities detract one from the luminous beauty of one's spirit. If all of one's time is spent on external things, the spirit may well become dried up and ugly. This is not to say that care should not be given to our physical

23

needs. A healthy spirit requires a dwelling place that is geared toward optimal health. It is very important to take care of the bodies God gave us for they are the housing in which our spirits live and the epitome of his creative gifts to us. To strive toward the highest degree of wellness that is attainable in all areas of life is essential. It is our duty to God and our responsibility to ourselves to seek appropriate medical treatment when it is needed and use maintenance, preventative and precautionary measures when they are indicated. Common sense tells us that these are important things to consider. The primary point to remember here is to watch carefully so that common sense will not develop into obsessive compulsions. With television, movies, popular magazines, "how to" books and other current techniques that the media uses, it is easy to get carried away into the development of the biggest and best self in the United States of America.

Living in today's society, with its strong emphasis on eternal youth, physical perfection and radiant external beauty, our pilgrims in the first mansion need to be cautious so that they will not become excessively involved in the allurements of the time. Health spas, beauty parlors, body building centers, elegant fashions, mysterious beauty fluids, and elaborate resorts that promise to change gray, wrinkles, and fat to the ultimate new look guaranteed to dazzle and delight, can be over used very easily. Because they are the popular trend, they are the "in" thing to do. Trends exist in every area of development. When one is feverishly racing about from place to place, trying to keep up with the latest fads, it is easy to see how the essentials of the spiritual life can slip into the background and take an unimportant place in one's daily existence. Prudence warns our pilgrims to keep the current craze in perspective. This virtue also aids our pilgrims so that they will not be conned into becoming trapped in the promise of great expectations. The majority of such promises come up empty. What is wrong with gray and wrinkles anyway?

Our first mansion lies at the outer edge of the castle. It has many, many rooms, as we already know, and it also has many, many people. Before our pilgrims begin their walk around this mansion, let them first stand for a few moments and gaze quietly through the windows to the dark lands outside. They see many shadowy shapes on the land. This tells our pilgrims that it is very populated. They find people who are intensely entangled in the many commodities of modern society and whose main purpose in life is to keep up with the latest and become the greatest in the eyes of the world. God does not exist for them. The people outside the castle are frantically involved in a multitude of external pursuits and do not have the time for him. Their lives are grounded in the pleasure principle. Instant gratification is the name of the game: I want what I want when I want it, and I want it now. Their lives are based on wants, which stress greed, power, control and riches, rather than on needs. The more they get, the more they want. "Let me take advantage of you," they mutter inaudibly. Not only does this indicate a nonexistent spiritual life, but also an extremely low level of psychological and emotional maturity. The lands stretching far and wide outside the castle walls are populated with many groups of these people. They are not aware of a personal, loving God. "Me-ism" is where it is. There is no realization of a life that goes beyond the here and now or of a life where things are not seen, smelled, touched, tasted or heard. There is no experience of a call to something that goes beyond oneself. Giving with no reward attached to it seems absurd. A favor for a favor reigns. The element of the spiritual has not been abstracted and realized as a distinct area of growth. A spiritual orientation based on living the teachings of Jesus without compromise seems ridiculous. There is no ability to enter within oneself or seek beyond oneself. Teresa saw these people as seriously ill, critically sick and acutely diseased. They are disabled in the severest and fullest sense of the word. She likened them to the vilest creatures that could ever be imagined. It would be a safe assumption to say that the people who live outside the castle would need to be stopped in their tracks by the Lord himself in order to realize that there is a door to the castle and a rich abundant life inside.

Now let us turn aside from our window gazing. Our pilgrims want to begin their walk through the outer rooms of the first mansion! They find that these rooms are very populated too. That is because many Christians get no further than this mansion. They spend their whole lives here because they are very much absorbed and attached to things of a temporal nature. They remain engrossed in the pleasures and vanities of the world. However, the people here have occasional good desires. They support the Church and what she teaches in a general way. Occasionally they read books of a spiritual nature. Now and then they give some thoughts to God. Two or three times during the year they experience warm flashes of fervent faith, usually at Christmas and Easter, which commonly are brief in time and intensity. Many inhabitants of the first mansion are a few steps above the water, rice, and mud Christians who darken the door of the

Church by their own volition only once in their lives. The other two times they are brought in, cradled in the arms of their parents, or rolled in on a catafalque. At times these Christians think seriously about their spiritual lives and say memorized or formal prayers sometimes without attention, but very intense prayers are said in times of personal crisis. Now and then these people dabble in meditation, but they are easily pulled away by their concerns in the world. They seem to walk on the razor's edge, sometimes falling into mortal sin and sometimes giving serious thoughts about remaining in a state of grace. Their fingers are very much hooked into the world. They still seek its honors, ambitions, glamour, glitter, pleasures, false values and vanities. If they are not careful, they can become obsessed by their possessions, jealousies, trivialities, or personal dignity. They can easily become unscrupulous busybodies, slanderous gossips, or conceited snobs. If a person will notice, each one of these behaviors, other negative traits, and each concern in the world that is not of God, are characterized by Teresa as numerous ghastly creatures that lurk closely around the outside of the castle. They take on many symbolic forms that send chills up one's spine. Some are very familiar. Cockroaches, cunning jungle animals, stink bugs, mosquitoes, rattlesnakes, tarantulas, scaly reptiles, and other types of nasty, unwelcome creatures that one cares not to meet up with very often are represented. These creatures not only stalk the outside of the castle, they are also encountered frequently in the peripheral rooms of the first mansion.

The heat and light from the center of the castle reaches this mansion in a faint and diffuse form. The darkness is made more grotesque by the presence of these hideous vermin and other varmints that lie hidden in the shadowy corners of the rooms. All is cold and dim. Mortal sin permeates the air with its putrid odor. These rooms are very poor because their inhabitants tend to slide into mortal sin very easily. These rooms are also very sad. There is only an occasional glimpse of happiness and light. These are made by the strong pilgrims who decide to push onward through the mansion and distance themselves from the outer rooms. These glimpses are rare, since the majority of people feel no urge to move and block out the light of God by their own lack of will and lack of motivation.

Every sin is a personal and social degradation. Suffering became part of the human condition after the first sin. The person who deliberately sins does not use God's gift of free will in a responsible manner. He or she chooses to offend God, refuses to love, abuses one's personhood, hurts others and adds to the agonies of humanity. Teresa saw mortal sin as the ultimate evil in life. When an individual is in a state of mortal sin, there is deprivation of God's friendship, total loss of his life and love, and supernatural death to one's spirit. An individual's spiritual life is as viable as a pile of cold gray ash. A person becomes darker than the darkest dark in this state. All the good works one may do are to no avail. They are absolutely worthless. The good works are neither pleasing to God, since there is an estrangement from him, nor do they help in the attainment of heaven since grace is nonexistent in the person. Teresa compares a person who, through his own fault, withdraws from God, to a small spring that is black and foul smelling. All the water coming from this spring is filthy and wretched, and everything it touches becomes dirty and contaminated. A perfect example of the effects of pollution in all its forms! She likens a person bright with God's love to a tiny crystal clear spring. Everything the fresh, clean water touches reflects verdant growth and abundant harvest. As the sun shines on both the clean and dirty waters, so does God shine his love on those who love him and those who have turned away from him. Those who love him reflect his love as in a mirror and continue to grow in his love. Those who have turned away are like objects that are covered with thick tar. God's love glistens radiantly on them, but they are unaware of it since they are encrusted in their own sticky blackness.

Two prerequisites for prayer

When our pilgrims decide to journey from the outer rooms to the interior dwellings of the first mansion, they must be prepared to spend long lengths of time in two very important rooms. Both are large and are essential requirements before advancement can be made into the second mansion. Successful passage through these rooms helps our pilgrims to see through the vanities, pleasures, riches and honors of the world that were so prevalent in the outer rooms just left behind.

The first room is the room of humility. The first mansion draws its name from this room. It is called the mansion of humility. This virtue is essential on the spiritual journey for it gives sincere pilgrims the desire to see themselves as they stand before God. Humility is the forerunner of all the virtues. There is a couplet from an Irish poem that expresses this beautifully:

Humility that low, sweet root
From which all heavenly virtues shoot.

When one seeks a true Christian example of humility, one need only look to Mary, the mother of Jesus. The style of living Mary pursued was immersed in "being" for God. She was the true reed of God, for she had no murmurings in her mind that would block or alter God's will for her. Mary was tranquil and still when she pondered in her heart all that was done for her. She thought about all of these events with an awesome wonder. In her home at Nazareth, she was content to be quietly anonymous and purely receptive to receiving God's word. Mary's interior silence brought her in contact with her true self, the center of her being, where God dwells. She made no fuss, nor did she make any speeches about being the mother of God. Mary saw herself in relation to herself and in relation to God. This is why her response to God was complete and total. Her humility was like a quiet light, warm and ever present to God and others. She did not let herself be swayed by anything except what God preferred.

Teresa gives us a sound and sure distinction between true humility and false humility. When we have true humility we are not troubled or disturbed in our deepest center. We experience peace, joy and tranquility even in the midst of great inner turmoil and trials. We do not wish to lose this interior stillness for it makes the heart grow in love and gives us the desire and the knowledge to serve God better. Humility helps us strive in the best way possible toward what seems to be right. We do the best we can with what we have and leave the rest to God. True humility passes unnoticed between God and the individual. It develops through a profound awareness of our sinfulness and nothingness before God.

False humility gives us unrest in the heart. Sometimes it is similar to a great ruckus rumbling inside us. An unrest in the heart leads to a distrust in God and in others. This humility is not for God alone because it takes something back with it to nourish false pride. False humility is superficial and can be used to control or manipulate. It is a humility with hooks so to speak.

Teresa warns sincere seekers who are advanced in the first mansion that it is easy to get caught up in their newly found journey and go into a tumultuous expression of religious activities that are unwise at this moment and at any other moment. Pilgrims can easily get involved in spiritual practices which are performed in an imprudent manner. In this mansion such things are unwise for those who are barely beginning the spiritual journey. Intense spiritual activities smack of false humility. Self-gratification is still very much a part of their personhood at this stage.

It needs to be fed, and this desire is fulfilled through a heavy involvement with anything that may be spiritual. Selfish gratification is like blood-sucking insects that drain life. Intense activities can be a rationalized form of self-gratification. If not recognized and stopped, they can lead to deep trouble. Excessive penance and immoderate self-abnegation can ruin health. Over-zealous activities can turn mole hills into mountains and can also be disconcerting to other people. Scruples can develop from nitpicking at small faults. Spiritual activities can also wind one up so tight that the relaxation that is necessary for the reception of God's gentle graces is not present. There must be a constant guard against these things because they cause serious harm in all areas of human development. Teresa warns all that the interior peace of other people who are in the house where one lives is to be safeguarded at all costs. She holds mutual love in high esteem and this is always to be respected. True perfection, she cautions, consists in loving God and loving others. All else serves as a means for protecting this love. When a person truly loves, real humility is always at work. This can be illustrated by watching a bee at work making honey in the beehive. The bee is giving his all and doing that for which his Creator made him. Nothing bothers or disturbs him. Every part of his job is done well, yet he is not driven by perfection. He does not work to receive love and attention. He is not driven by compulsion or competition, nor does he use work as a distraction from other life necessities. It is easy to see that without humility in one's life many things go wrong. Without humility an individual easily gets tangled up in the various components that make up a work task or activity. There is fussing, fuming and complaining all around. This is a far cry from doing work attentively, with energy, and with good humor. Humility is well integrated into the work when tasks are completed in this way.

Teresa tells her pilgrims that the most necessary room in the first mansion is the room of self-knowledge. The pilgrim first becomes aware of self-knowledge in this room, and this awareness then grows and grows throughout the journey within the interior castle. Oh, look! There is the busy bee again. Now he tells our pilgrims about self-knowledge. Our bee friend is buzzing around, gathering nectar from all the flowers. See how he goes from flower, to flower, to flower? So must the individuals be in the room of self-knowledge, which has so many places to visit and ponder the grandeur of God. As the inhabitants ruminate upon the great mysteries and majesty of God, they discover their own lowliness. Here, they really taste the sweetness of God's mercy, for it is only through his mercy that self-knowledge can be put into practice. Our pilgrims gradually loosen the very strong hold they had on the things of the world and the things of self that did not speak of God, as they grow to realize how much God's help is needed. They become more aware of their sins, faults, and infidelities and grow in the knowledge of what is good and what is evil. Our pilgrims are just beginning to gradually learn to see things the way God intends them to be seen.

Many people do not even make it to this room in the first mansion. They do not because they would rather amble around in the doldrums content to remain absorbed in their own affairs. They proceed with their ordinary daily routine, going from one task to another in a mediocre frame of mind. These people are very much satisfied with the way things are. The sameness requires nothing from them. They go about very consoled because they need not take a risk, meet a challenge, or strive beyond the known. The complacency of dullness is all they desire. They never create a ripple on their pool of life.

The room of self-knowledge requires a certain amount of seeing life beyond oneself. It is seeing life as it really is, that is, as coming from God. The individuals in this room are just beginning to see themselves as they stand before God. At this stage of the spiritual journey, this takes a lot of grit. The layers of self are just beginning to be removed, and this can be a painful and frightening experience. A person's protective coating is slowly being taken away. Needless to say, the room of self-knowledge must be lived in for a lengthy stretch of time before any real progress can be made. To place self and God in proper perspective puts a pilgrim on the right road so that the continuing journey will be on a safe and level path. If the stay in this room is short, the self is still padded in a thick, cumbersome, protective coat, and the person has not yet learned to rely on the mercy of God. The big, important self is flying about like some frenzied maniac all aflutter with where one is going and what one is doing. There is a complex schedule of what an individual wants to do, and when, and where. A person would certainly meet a disastrous end if not enough time was spent in this room. Self-knowledge only comes through knowing God. He increases while the self decreases. When looking at his grandeur, one sees oneself as a microbe against the universe. When looking at his goodness one sees one's own misery. In seeing self in this way a pilgrim strives to transcend. There is a pull to be freed from one's own mire of misery toward the goodness of God. It is a pull from the black waters mentioned earlier. This time the black waters include names like fear, weakness, cowardice, and faintness of heart. The black waters can also entrap an individual by a constant reflection on the uncertainties of the future journey. A person's self proposes many things. The person watches others to see if he or she is being watched. What would they say if they knew where I was headed? If I take this path, will things go badly? What would I do if pride caused me to take the first step? If I continue this journey, how will I cope with the effects of lofty mystical prayer? Will I be judged better than others if a separate path is taken? If, if, if. . . This could go on and on forever and really cause havoc with one's stability. All these fears do not stem from true self-knowledge, nor do they stem from true humility. If these questions must be asked, the self has not been understood. There is a lack of freedom from self and a distortion of self. One should consider what happens in the room of humility if these questions persist. In order to overcome self, Teresa challenges her pilgrims to place their eyes on Christ and his saints, for only then is self-knowledge learned. Self-knowledge is not for the weak of heart.

The first mansion is a very precarious place in which to be. The ability of the majority of the inhabitants in relating to others is limited by their own wants. As the fog and damp wrap themselves around everything within the outer rooms, so are the inhabitants wrapped up in themselves and their own concerns. They are only able to develop acquaintances from whom they can get things. This mansion is really an anteroom to the castle, because these people see themselves as the center of their own world. Even though they have some desires not to offend God and perform some good works, they can easily journey right back outside the castle door. Many loathsome creatures that represent the wiles and deceits of all things evil, come in through this door and creep around in the darkness of the first mansion. They lie in wait to jump on or bite any unsuspecting inhabitants.

The sincere pilgrims who desire to pursue the path to higher mansions must realize that they are weak at this beginning point in their spiritual journey. Teresa advises them to take Mary and the saints as their strong intercessors. Through them they will gain strength and will not have to fight alone. These pilgrims will then be the shafts of light that break up the darkness and gloom of the first mansion as they bravely march through it.

Second Mansion

THE ENTRANCE TO THE CASTLE

Our second mansion is the official door by which entrance is made into the castle proper. The transport is made via prayer. The people who enter here are those who have begun a sincere practice of prayer and realize how important this practice is within their lives. They begin in earnest to give themselves to God. God attracts them, and they respond by attending to him through daily vocal and mental prayer. Their prayer is no longer an occasional memorized prayer that is said by rote. It has developed a deeper realm. External prayer, which often was words that quickly flashed from the mind then out of the mouth has become internalized. Vocal prayer begins to make a loving detour through the heart. The descent into the heart puts the heart into action. Saying prayers has developed into a state of being which is beginning to be based on a prayerful presence. Our pilgrims become more conscious of God during the times outside of prayer.

In the mansion our pilgrims find that they are very new students who are acquiring knowledge about the art of prayer. The pilgrims learn about prayer through the senses. They read about it, hear about it, talk about it, see it in various forms, and feel good about doing it. The pilgrims are slowly becoming aware of the first stages of mental prayer. There is a gradual movement from an emphasis on reasoning and analysis in prayer to prayer that comes from the heart. Prayer at this early stage is a giving of time. The pilgrims make firm resolutions to give God specific times of the day which will be set aside for prayer. They learn various methods and techniques that place the mind on God. The pilgrims attend workshops, seminars, retreats, and conferences on topics regarding the many aspects of prayer and praying. They find that prayer is an insatiable hunger, it is stimulating, it is delightful, and it can lead to great desires.

There is a grave danger in these great desires. Our pilgrims have found that prayer can be a pleasant and attractive experience. Because of this delight, they want to experience it at its highest level. They romanticize about hidden colloquies with God and seek the *crème de la crème* of the prayer experience. They want to learn the secrets of the mystics. These pilgrims who are filled with such lofty desires would do well to remember the location of the second mansion. It is still on the periphery of the castle. People here must be content with their place in prayer formation. To journey off into flights of fancy through an overactive imagination and think oneself as the greatest of mystics would never do. A person is not to shoot for the stars and pose like a statue of Teresa in ecstasy and expect instant rapture because he or she has taken that pose. There are no quick and easy routes on the road of prayer. There is no magic formula for instant mysticism. The secret here is to remain in the present moment. The pilgrims should strive to keep mind and body together and desire to be content with where they are at this moment in time. The pilgrimage on the path of prayer can prove to be long and arduous. The passage of time will bring this to a harsh reality. At the present moment, our pilgrims are very much in the honeymoon stage of prayer. Everything is wonderful and fascinating. This is a time to float in the beauty of prayer and take pleasure in the fresh delights that it brings. May our hasty pilgrims calm down, relax, and enjoy the newness of it all, for alas, they will discover in time that prayer is not all sweetness and light.

Entrance into the second mansion is like a rebirth. An exploration into God has begun. There is a true awakening and a new coming to life that was not present before. God becomes a real and viable part of daily life. This spiritual regeneration resembles a second birth. As the spiritual life becomes more apparent, there is a gradual shift in one's priorities which indicates that new values are emerging. In the second mansion our pilgrim is gradually realizing that self-worth is not dependent on what a person owns, earns, produces, or achieves. This realization goes contrary to what modern society and the media tend to emphasize. The pilgrim begins to see that the spiritual life will be opposed to many things he or she felt comfortable with before his or her journey in prayer began. The pilgrim also begins to see that who a person is and the way he or she lives is more important than what a person does. There is an explorer's interest in this new realm of the pilgrim's life. It is a realm that broadens one's perspective about life. Our excited pilgrim is eager to investigate this unknown and mysterious territory. Before beginning the trek, however, some necessary staples must be taken along in order to sustain life along the journey.

Our ardent pilgrims need a few strong internal traits if the trek through the second mansion is to be successful. One indispensable trait is determination. It is essential if the pilgrims are to make progress because they can very easily slip and fall back into the first firm decision to avoid all things that go against God's merciful love is needed. Pilgrims find that it is very easy to fall into many traps that lead to offending God. A journey through these rooms involves as much effort as was needed to walk through the populated thoroughfare of the first mansion. The difference here is that the pilgrims are aware of the spiritual realm, and the many dangers are not as threatening because they are recognized for what they are. There is also a great hope to progress farther along and eventually reach the center of the castle. Yes, the journey has begun in earnest and our pilgrims are nearer to the Lord than before. It is easier to hear his words because there is not as much screaming and screeching from the wild creatures as there was in the first mansion. Jesus is a closer neighbor than before. The individual pilgrims are seeking to learn about the life and teachings of their new neighbor in order to become more like him. His voice comes to them through good sermons, good books, good conversations, and good friends. All these things help them to grow in and through the second mansion. They also begin to see God calling through things that were repugnant before. Illnesses and hardships, and yes, even lukewarm prayers slowly initiate our pilgrims into harmony with the incarnate Christ. These events, which were considered in the negative before, are now new experiences for our pilgrims. Within this new context, they soon find that these experiences too are a part of learning to be like Jesus. Determination is manifested through a courageous strength of will that recognizes but rises above feelings of helplessness and fear.

Determination requires a generous spirit. We learn to give without expecting things in return. We have a firm desire to progress even when we know there will be trouble spots along the way. In our eagerness to ⁓n about the ways of God, we are continually thinking about what to ¹⁓r to go forward on the spiritual path. We are learning to know ⁼ng more and more like Jesus. A great dimension within ⁓ the Sacrament of Reconciliation and taking contri- ⁓." goes beyond what has been done and is ⁓ds to be a firm resolve not to do those ⁼ go against love again. This requires ρpropriate precautionary measures to avoided. We are healed through our ⁓rgiveness. When the priest forgives our ⁼ruly forgiven. After we are absolved we ⁼ need to go moping about with a load of needless neurotic guilt or senseless anxiety about our past sins. Jesus forgives us through the words of the priest. It is important for us to forgive the negatives within ourselves and to forgive other people who may have acted against us. We forgive them and they forgive us. True forgiveness of trusted, loved ones takes time. We must be healed in all dimensions of our personalities. Then we can grow without guilt or other reminders of how dear ones have hurt us. Our forgiveness from God goes hand in hand with how we forgive ourselves, our family, friends, acquaintances, enemies and those of other cultures, societies and nations.

Patience must also accompany our pilgrims on their journey. Since they are but neophytes on the spiritual path, they should not expect great things to happen along the road in the second mansion. They may be greatly inspired by the special events that happen in the lives of saintly people about whom they are reading in spiritual books. It would be an error, though, if they ardently long for these same events to happen to them at the present time, or at other times in the future. Special events that come from God are given to people in the context of their place in history and the customs of their society. People are different and God treats them accordingly, so it is a mistake to desire what a certain saint received from God in the forms of his extraordinary gifts. God gives to each person according to each one's individuality. To expect any type of extraordinary gift from God at this point on the spiritual journey would be like building the foundation of the spiritual life on sand. One little uneventful shake would bring the building crashing down to the ground. If pilgrims really want what God wants, patience would give them the contentment to be where they are in their spiritual development. Virtues are just beginning to grow. There are a thousand faults and failings with which to contend. They are all like reptiles and rodents running along the beginner's path. All these pesky varmints are jumping on our neophytes, biting them and sticking to their skin. It is difficult to get rid of many of these little creatures!

The pilgrims in the second mansion are like spiritual seeds that have just been planted. They are experiencing the first stages of germination underneath the soil. Their roots are just beginning to grow in God. Growth will come if there is a determination and a patience to go forward within God's parameters. The warm energy of the sun, which symbolizes God, cannot be seen or felt in its full intensity because the seeds just are not ready for it. Yet, the warm energy from the sun that is absorbed by the soil will give the seeds courage and strength to grow in times of trial.

Yes, trials begin midway through the second mansion. At this stage frequently it seems as if our pilgrims are being torn asunder. Sometimes our pilgrims want to proceed into the unknown. At other times they want to turn back and forget it all. During the pilgrims' times of weakness, self-indulgent pleasures of the world are remembered well. The hollow vainglories of the life just left tug and pull. "Come back," they relentlessly urge. "Come back to where life was nothing but fun, fun, fun." Memories of bawdy parties entice and tempt. The pilgrims ruminate about popularity, wealth and status among the jet set, or luxuries, comforts, and pleasures with the "in" group. There were no difficult decisions to make then. They did not have to think about anybody except themselves. It seems as if the empty allurements of their past lives have risen from the fog. They are now clamping their sinister delights on our pilgrims with a strong, vice-like grip. The pilgrims feel as if they are going to be pulled back into the murky depths. Here pilgrims hold an ambivalent attitude. There is a fear that religion will interfere with their life styles, their freedom and their health. During these times they seem to vacillate and hesitate. Which would be the best way to go?

Teresa never said it would be easy, but she gives us hope and inspiration and tells us not to falter when trials come. She strongly encourages perseverance in prayer and reliance on the mercy of God during times of tribulation.

Perseverance is very necessary in the second mansion. Many gains are made by it. In the second mansion the evil one is very busy trying to pull our good pilgrims back into the grime of the world. If he succeeds, he will be very happy because then the pilgrims will, again, be unable to hear the voice of God and unable to speak of his goodness. They will, once more, become blind to the loving gaze of God and deaf to his words. On the other hand, if their perseverance is sound, the influence of the devil is not as strong as he may think. The pilgrims resist him more. Their resistance has strengthened because they have been diligent in pursuing God. The intellect is more developed through faith. The senses are more refined by acknowledging the beauty of God. When they are compared to that for which the pilgrims are now striving, they know, through reason, that their previous shabby life styles were not worth much. Memory reminds them that all earthly gains come to an abrupt end. Death ends all temporal pursuits and it comes unexpectedly, as a thief in the night. Soon after death, the person is probably forgotten. Decay invades the corpse and the remains rot away. Now it is known that the joy felt while pursuing things that were not of God was filled with contradictions, insecurities and discord. Our pilgrims would not want to visit the houses outside of the castle because the blessings and gifts from God were not experienced there. Yes, the pilgrims hear the cries of the godless world, but their steadfast persistence in pursuing the spiritual urges them forward.

A lack of perseverance in the second mansion can abruptly terminate the spiritual journey and cause an individual to run out the door and into the world. If a person no longer tries, there is failure. The defeat comes from within. A weakness of purpose leaves insurmountable barriers. In order to strive forward one must grit one's teeth and doggedly march on.

God's mercy will aid the pilgrim during hard times. His mercy will help one to recognize the deceptions along the way and encourage one not to give up when things go wrong. Without the mercy of God, nothing can be done, the journey ceases. A pilgrim keeps going with mercy in his or her heart. With God's gentle compassion within, an individual realizes that true enlightenment only comes from a journey inside the castle.

As the pilgrims proceed further along in the second mansion, they experience dryness, negative thoughts and other distractions in prayer. These are new little reptiles with which to do combat. Teresa said that they are to be considered as part of God's plan for the pilgrims. These little critters may pursue them relentlessly throughout the spiritual journey. It appears as if our pilgrims are unable to chase them away! Teresa gives comforting words here. She says not to be alarmed or disturbed if there are wanderings in the mind. No matter how ridiculous distractions may be, our pilgrims should not cling to them, deliberately push them away, or get upset by them. Distractions will come and go. Just laugh at them and stay quiet in God. Our pilgrims remember that the will is the master of the situation. The will should bring the mind gently and quietly back to prayer.

When walking through the rooms of the second mansion we soon find out that love is a choosing. We are gradually learning that love requires decisions if it is to grow. We make these decisions each day. We find that love goes beyond a mood, a happy sensation, a delightful experience, a contented feeling, or an inner, warm glow. We find that love comes from a conscience that is accurate, educated and in accord with the teachings of the Church. Loving God must be conscious choices directed toward him even when there is no attraction to love him, ourselves, or others and there is a strong attraction to the pleasures of the here and now that are not of God.

Let us look at an example. An overweight young man is seated at a sumptuous banquet. His weight problem is directly connected with over-eating. The delicious array of the various dishes are a delight to his eyes. The savory aroma that drifts from them assails his nostrils. The palatable foods present before him make his mouth water. Grace has been said and the many platters begin circulating around the table. The first plate reaches our young man. He takes the large serving utensil and digs in. Wait! Hold everything! He has a decision to make if his mind is properly motivated according to love's choosing. Will he fill his plate with moderate proportions or even small helpings in order to take preventative steps concerning the body God gave him? Will he gorge himself to ultimate exhaustion, not giving two cents worth of a thought to the excess poundage he will be packing on his already ponderous frame? The choice is his. It will be made on his ability to respond to love. In this case, it not only includes God's love, but also a respectful love for self. When we are faced with a little or big decision, task or event that is difficult or displeasing to us but a conscious choice toward love, we find that saying the heart phrase "All for Jesus" makes things go easier.

Choosing love becomes easier when it is not isolated in the mind but merged with the heart where God dwells. Here it becomes joined with God's wishes and bonded with his strength. God does for us what we are unable to do by ourselves. In this way we become servants to love. Teresa is fond of the title, "Servant of Love." In the second mansion we realize the significant beauty of this title for the first time. We become aware of its true meaning. The realization of the greatness of God's love, and that this love is really present in our hearts, is astonishing. God's love in our hearts is above our own ability to love, but there is no separateness between the two. In the second mansion it is through this love that pilgrims are given the strength to make a sincere effort to wean them-selves away from the things of the world. As their journey through this mansion reaches its end, the sincerity of this intent is manifested by living as if everything comes from a radiance of this love. The pilgrims become faithful and charitable. There is a kindness and gentleness, an honesty and courage in the face of life. They try to choose against self-love, discour-agement, failure and the attraction for the here and now. Even though the journey through the second mansion is almost completed, pilgrims have bad habits to overcome and false values to be put in their appropriate place. Many weaknesses are present. The ways of love are chosen more often here because there is a strengthening of virtues and an adherence to prayer. The journey through the second mansion has been long and balanced with both delightful and difficult times. It has been well worth the effort put forth. The beauty of God's graces urges our pilgrims onward. The exuberance of new beginnings, which were felt so intensely at the beginning of this mansion, are slightly less intense. Yet there is still the desire to seek and find where the King of Glory dwells.

Life in the second mansion can prove to be a dissonant experience if a person is not careful. The incongruence stems from the fact that an individual has not really "settled in" within the spiritual life yet. He or she has just begun this process. There are many trials and errors. There are many firm resolutions made which end up broken after a few months in practice, much like the proverbial New Year's resolutions. Often unfulfilled desires can cause a person to over react. One meets discouragement and depression along the way. If our pilgrims are watchful and mindful of the difficulties along the road, they can see that even from falls God can draw out good. When pilgrims stumble in the second mansion they should not be disconsolate. They just stop on their journey and spend some time pondering their problems in the light of God's mercy. If they slide back into the slime of life outside the castle, are they to go about and weep and wail and gnash their teeth? What did Jesus say to the woman who was caught committing adultery? Did he give her a scornful look? Did he mention that she should lament forever? Quite the contrary. It was a simple phrase said with much love and tenderness. "I do not condemn you, go now and sin no more," shows the deep compassion Jesus holds for all. One errs, realizes the error, is sorry for it, then is brought back to God and reconciled with him. Through reconciliation our pilgrims see the great harm they have done. The damage is intensified because the all-powerful love of God has been experienced before the transgressions took place. After reconciliation they become at peace with God. A relapse into their former lives causes our pilgrims to rely more profoundly on the great mercy of God and have less trust in themselves. If they forget their daily prayers, as an example, they are sorry and begin again. To begin again is to return to the peace within the castle. It is another returning to God. Jesus never leaves the one who struggles in the uncertainties of an unknown way. He is the way. He shows us how to love God our Father. He is not only our pilgrim's new neighbor but also our pilgrim's best friend. No person could find a better friend even if he or she could walk the earth for a thousand years.

Even when we reach the end of the second mansion, we still have been on the spiritual journey for just a short time. We can only seek to do small things for God. We try not to be impatient about what lies ahead. God knows what is best and he does not need a negotiator or a consultant regarding what he should do. At this stage Teresa exhorts us to labor and be resolute and prepare with all possible diligence to bring our will into conformity with the will of God. A very important point, for it leads to the greatest perfection attainable on the spiritual journey. If we err in this, that is, preferring our own will instead of God's, it would be like building our spiritual house with feathers. Nothing holds it together, and when a small breeze comes . . . poof, there is nothing.

La voluntad de Dios

In the second mansion we learn how to take the spiritual life seriously. The will of God increases in importance and becomes a necessary guidepost to mark our way. Let us stop on our journey and rest for a while. During our brief pause, we will ponder that often used phrase, "the will of God." What precisely does it mean?

The will of God is not a consolation prize that is passively accepted after all possible resources have been exhausted. It is not a dead end that presents itself after doing what is best has been done in any given situation. The will of God is not something to say when there are no other alternatives. It is not a pious excuse used to explain away the unexplainable, nor is it a catch phrase used in order to put limits on the courage that may be needed when we are stepping into unknown situations or coping with new experiences. God's will is not concentration camps, car accidents, or any other evil, tragic, or stupid circumstance of humanity. God's will is found in accepting, with trust and love, the consequences in our lives and listening with hope to what they are teaching us. When we locate the ingredients for our spiritual growth within the circumstances in our lives, we are doing his will. This is important to remember on our castle journey. Stated quite simply, the will of God is love. It is the means by which we embrace and enter into the most intimate relationship with the triune God.

God made us free to think and know and to love and choose. He does not force us to do anything. There is no automatic operation of his will in us. Teresa said that everything we gain comes from what we are able to give. She confirms this by noting that God does not give himself totally to us until we give ourselves totally to him. Embracing God's will is made by giving our human will to him and letting him work in the events of our lives. To submit to this is no easy matter. It requires continual dyings and risings. It takes a cheerful abandonment of self. It demands visualizing events and occurrences within God's presence. It calls for looking at everything that stems from faith with love. It is a way in which we live by faith, faith, faith. It is a continual going beyond our own needs, thoughts, desires, ideas, and rising above our grudges, pet peeves, preju- dices, likes and dislikes, judgments, strong opinions and other non-essen- tials that muddle the mind. It is a letting go combined with a resting and letting God.

The ongoing, unfolding will of God involves continuous, conscious choices from us. These choices are based on love. We desire to accept whatever events come along in our lives with love. We know God's plan is revealed to us when we find elements for our spiritual growth in these events and in these choices. This is no easy task! A practical application is to see everything as Jesus might have seen it then respond as he would have responded. This takes some doing! When events and circumstances get unbearable, it is wise and a great help to focus our attention on Jesus in the Garden of Gethsemane. Then we can share the pain, share the fear, and share all other concerns with a loving friend who sincerely knows what we are going through in life. It would be comforting to keep a visual image in our minds of Jesus in the garden, or Jesus on the cross during difficult times that cause much worry. Sometimes it is all we can do to just hang on tightly to that rock, or hang on tightly to that cross with him! We hold tight and keep repeating in our minds, "Your will, not mine." Teresa consoles us by reminding us about what God gave to his best beloved. Teresa goes on to show how we can understand what God's will is. Sometimes it presents great trials, but God gives in proportion to the love he bears us. He also gives in accordance with the courage that he sees in each one of us. The courage must flow from the love we have for him. Teresa goes straight to the heart of the matter. She points to love. If we really love God, our love then shows how we bear the crosses he sends, no matter what the size. We are able to endure great things that seem beyond our strength when they are done with great love and in union with Jesus. It is Jesus who offers our will to the Father.

We know that God's will can be present in difficult and demanding things. We also realize, and this is very important, that his will is found in things that give us happiness and joy. Both create a well-balanced framework of the actions of God in our lives. This is good since there is then a symmetrical flowing of the sorrows and joys in our existence. When the awareness of symmetry is apparent within a person, it radiates out a quietness and simplicity of manner. These two elements are present in both the mind and the body. An overall gentleness, which grows through an ever greater opening to God's love, gives one a composure that calms and heals and shows God is very real. The person focuses on the good in others. He or she offers acceptance that welcomes others to be themselves with a good feeling, calls forth what is best in them and sees them as unique gifts from the Lord. This individual is one to whom others can speak frankly, for he or she values them and treats them with respect.

A person living God's will manifests a holy countenance even though he or she does not speak about God or things of a spiritual nature. An individual is immensely loveable and beautiful and his or her presence is sacramental. God is radiating from a person as the bright light shines from the sun. With this perspective, an individual really enjoys to the full the little surprises that mark each day. If these surprises are seen with the eyes of God, everything takes on a more brilliant beauty. His love unfolds everywhere: the quiet of the early morning, the cool breeze in the afternoon, the cloud formations at dusk, the splendor of a brilliant sunset, the rainbows sparkling in the dewdrops on the grass, the delicacy of a beautiful spring flower, a smiling friend, and understanding that goes beyond words, the giggles of the children, the twinkle within and crinkles around the eyes of the old folks, the majesty of a thunderstorm, a look of utmost tenderness, the eucharistic celebration.

Within the documents of Vatican II we find how the will of God is to be expressed. The Constitution on the Church states that: "All Christians in the conditions, duties, and circumstances of their lives, and through all these, will sanctify themselves more and more if they receive all things with faith, from the hands of the heavenly Father, and cooperate with the divine will, thus showing forth in that temporal service, the love with which God has loved the world" (41).

A delightful broadening of human relationships await an individual in the second mansion. Here is where the warm beginnings of spiritual friendships start. It is a new form of relating that has been previously unknown. Teresa places her wholehearted seal of approval on friendships that are rooted in God. Soul friends can be very supportive and comforting along the spiritual journey. It would be beneficial to converse with those who are further along on the spiritual path. A word of caution is necessary here. The pilgrim in the second mansion is to remember that all the experiences here are rather new and somewhat overwhelming. The pilgrim is still covered with faults, bad habits, inconsistencies, failings and other negative items that shade the power of God's gifts. One is unaware of these things.

The negative attributes attach to a person like an unseen leprosy. The delights of spiritual friends are refreshing and consoling to our pilgrim, but it would be imprudent to plunge head over heels into this new experience. There are several reasons for this. We can become totally engrossed in the new friend, and therefore forget God. We could use the new friend in order to get things, although this time the things are of a spiritual or religious nature. We could use the friend in order to try and obtain favors. We could desire to possess the new friend. The beauteous dawn of friendships in God has just risen to greet the day. To experience the full power of the ever increasing warmth of the sun is to experience spiritual friendship at its fullest extent. We must go forward slowly. God will grant his gifts to his friends that are rooted in him when the eyes of these friends are not on each other for the control of the other but focused directly on him.

Within one's relationships inside the second mansion the pilgrim finds an attraction to a few people, and this is an experience that is new and pleasant on the spiritual road. There are the beginnings of a spiritual bonding. Frequently the attraction can have selfish desires. There is fear that these relationships will interfere with one's freedom, projects, productivity, independence, recreational pursuits, work, or busy schedule. On the other hand, the person finds that the pleasure and attractiveness are appealing and this leads him or her on. There is wonder, curiosity, and caution, but the caution is defeated by the desire to go forward and explore. At this stage, an individual is not yet open to spiritual vulnerability, sensitivity, or spontaneity.

The second mansion is a transitory place. An English Carmelite nun likened it to a train station. Everything is in a dither. The air is filled with the tensions of good-byes and desires to board the train which will take a person away from what he or she cares about and cherishes. It is a time of fear of losing temporal things that one has held dear while being active in worldly pursuits and a mysterious anticipation of what the upcoming journey to God will bring.

The pilgrim is anxious. The second mansion can be hard going. A person is not yet incorporated into a sound spiritual life. He or she has just begun to be remade in the Lord. A human being is constantly aware of his or her fragility. One resembles a lump of slippery, formless clay that is just taking shape in the Potter's hands. The light from the center of the castle is so enticing, yet it is still shaded, like a deep, smoky, red glow. A pilgrim finds that the mysterious drawing toward that fire remains entrancing even though he or she can only see it from a distance. Sometimes one feels alone and frightened. It is then that comfort is found in reflecting on the words of a poem written by another pilgrim who also felt alone, misunderstood and confused. He, too, was attracted to that same unquenching fire within.

> Lead, kindly Light, amid the encircling gloom,
> Lead thou me on;
> The night is dark, and I am far from home.
> Lead thou me on.
> Keep thou my feet; I do not ask to see
> The distant scene; one step enough for me.
>
> I was not ever thus, nor prayed that thou
> Shouldst lead me on;
> I loved to choose and see my path; but now
> Lead thou me on.
> I loved the garish day, and, spite of fears,
> Pride ruled my will; remember not past years.
>
> So long thy power hath blest me, sure it still
> Will lead me on
> O'er moor and fen, o'er crag and torrent, till
> The night is gone.
> And with the morn those angel faces smile,
> Which I have loved long since, and lost awhile.

John Henry Newman

Third Mansion

THE MANSION OF THE EXEMPLARY LIFE

Pilgrims who have just entered the third mansion have come through many difficulties. Through all their trials they have responded to grace and trusted in God. Teresa showers these pilgrims with great praise. She may have seen them as brave soldiers who, with the mercy of God, have fought the good fight and have won great battles. Happy are those pilgrim soldiers for they have not turned back! Happy are those pilgrim soldiers for they are now on a sound path that leads to salvation! It is through the winning of these battles that God gives these pilgrims a conscience that is grounded in him. This will remain so as long as the pilgrims do not abandon the path that leads through the third mansion.

Our third mansion was once referred to as the "mansion of the exemplary life," and rightly so, for it is the normal state of most good Christian people. These people are recognized as devout Catholics or good Christians. They have developed virtues and long not to offend God. There is an earnest avoidance of sin. They are fond of setting aside times for prayer and spend some time each day in recollection, both of which have become real needs. They do good works and help others. These people find a great satisfaction in doing things for God. They are able to show their love for God by loving their neighbors. They find more consolations in the spiritual life than they do in material comforts. They usually speak in an appropriate manner and dress modestly. They are adept at running their households and businesses or any other work they set out to do or in which they are involved. They have overcome many bad habits. In general, other people think they are just wonderful.

Jesus looks kindly upon the people in the third mansion who are moving ahead. He will not deny them entrance into the higher mansions if these travelers wish to proceed further. As our pilgrims walk around the third mansion, they find that it is a very large place. It is almost as large as the first mansion. They are also fascinated by the vast number of people. People are found in all areas of available space. They are especially found at the end of dead-end roads, in cul-de-sacs, and on the many side paths that wander off from the main route. There are great halls packed with people. The pilgrims also notice people in other passageways, auditoriums, chambers, gardens, vestibules, atriums and other nooks and crannies that are found in this mansion. Our pilgrims gasp in amazement! There are so many types of people that populate this mansion! From cardinals to chimney sweeps to case workers. From bishops to bellhops to ballerinas. They are quick to see that every possible life style is represented here. "Why?" our pilgrims question. They will soon find out.

It is very comfortable and cozy here in the third mansion. It is so comforting, in fact, that it drains any desire to push onward to the next mansion for most people. Many pilgrims on the spiritual journey have decided to settle down and sink their roots into the third mansion. They homestead here because they feel they have reached the verdant valleys of bliss and the flowery fields of spiritual repose. They feel they have reached the end of their spiritual journey. Everyone is very satisfied here. Everyone is greatly admired. Everything is very good.

Because this mansion seems so good it often serves as a stumbling block to true holiness. Although it tends to spiritually satisfy people, it is not the ultimate peak of the spiritual life. In order to find out why this mansion can be very dangerous through immobilization, let us look about and listen to some of the crowds that loiter around the various arcades.

Ah, what do we have here? It is a moderately sized palace within the third mansion named the palace of perfect persons. A whole cross section of humanity prevails herein. There are representatives from every walk of life. There are people from the armed forces and the government. There are professionals and unskilled workers. There are clergy and religious and kings and commoners. Everyone talks about how great these people are. Ah, but the sadness of it all is that these people believe every good word that is said about them. Because of these lavish praises, these people experience a decrease in awareness of their sinful natures. Sins no longer humiliate like they used to because these people rely heavily on what others tell them. They bury guilt, growing doubts and fears in order to achieve a state of self-satisfaction. They hardly realize they have faults, failings or bad habits. Their concept of God and his love are based on their own cognitive perceptions of him. He is a product of their reasoning. Since God is made in their image, it is easy to cope with him. There are no demands. God only hates what is vile and ugly and obtuse, and how can there be anything like that here where everything is so fine? All these people strive to stay away from sin, and because of this they expect God's love to be showered down upon them like a soft, spring rain. The people's interpretation of God's love is developed from their feeling of self-satisfaction. Self-satisfaction has evolved from doing good works, having good thoughts and desires, saying good prayers, expressing good actions, sending out good vibrations, being on their best behavior, and striving to be impeccable in every way. All their energies are directed toward what is good religious behavior. There is absolutely no stepping out of the lines of propriety here.

It is true that these people are trying to lead virtuous lives. The two problems here are that they have reduced God to their own cognitive models which they can understand, and that they are unaware of their own negative traits. All these traits are like weeds in a garden. A mower has come along and cut off the large visible foliage, but the dendritic roots are still deep within the soil. A selfishness results quite easily here. People put expectations on the God of their own creation. They do good things for God and then expect God to give good things to them in return. They also do not have the great shame that was present when they thought about their faults and failings in the past. Teresa was sensitive to this. She warns that pilgrims must watch carefully lest they fall into the error of thinking themselves greater than they really are just because the occasions for great faults have been removed. Large external negative traits may have been recognized and eliminated, but underneath subtle, insidious forms need to be searched for and destroyed. It is very easy to fall back into bad habits without realizing it. Weaknesses and moderate faults grow slowly when they are not faced squarely and dealt with willingly. Negative traits here do not spoil the external facade of the good person. However, they are very present and may be rationalized as good traits under the cover of religion. These people are usually unaware this is happening because they are overly concerned about their spiritual images and that brings deception. They concentrate so intensely on being good people here that the bad, although present, is forgotten. This is a classic case of being spiritually self-centered. Being so involved with becoming the perfect person in such a selfish way leads to a loss of true virtue. Holiness has become a fetish. These people consider themselves as very holy and they sincerely believe it.

If a person lived to be as old as Methuselah and sincerely tried to understand and conceptualize God during that time, his or her efforts would be fruitless. God is a mystery that far surpasses human cognition. Only he alone is holy. Only he alone is good. It is not the opinions of others that matter for they do not make an individual holy. It is only what

God thinks that matters. Look through his eyes instead of the eyes of others for a true picture of self. Look to Jesus for an example of a virtuous life. Look to the Holy Spirit for enlightenment in order to be able to see one's self as one really is.

In the third mansion we find several courtyards of complacency. They are also known as the great plateaus of the spiritual life. Many people remain on these plateaus until death. The first bright lights of God's love have been experienced in their lives. The white hot heat of their initial enthusiasm is now lukewarm. Restless urgings have subsided. The new has become routine. The thrill is gone. People find that their spiritual energy is at a low ebb. There is a lack of careful watching and these people have fallen right into mediocrity. People here are very involved with being good Christians. They trust and rely on their own strengths and accomplishments. This makes up for the great fervor that was once felt. All the good works they do compensate for the strong love they once felt they had for God. Because prayer is dull many times, they work harder and feel that their work is their prayer. Their prayer time basically consists in gaining indulgences, remaining in God's good favor and getting his graces. Their choices in life and things they do are directed toward saving their souls and gaining eternal salvation. This quickly develops into a false sense of security. The people think they love God because they do so much for him. Prayer has become an efficient, formal duty to get out of the way so that they can get on with their work for the day. These people may be called pillars of the parish or extraordinary workers for Jesus and are involved in every aspect of parish life. They have their favorite apostolates outside of the parish. They receive great compliments for their organizational skills. They may have a tendency to break their arms while patting themselves on their backs after a hectic day. Running around for Jesus is their motto. They are busy, busy, busy. They are content in their busyness. It makes them feel important and worthwhile. What actually happens here is that their spiritual scale has become unbalanced. Their previous scale was equalized between being with God and doing for him. Now there is an emphasis on doing for God. Retreats, recollection, silence and solitude, or any other activity that causes them to stop and reflect are put on the back burner.

Initially these activities were good and helpful, but now they are mundane and done only if the person feels inspired to do them. Who needs a quiet, introspective look at self and one's relationship with God when so much of God's work needs to be done? This is their easy rationalization. The well-scheduled days of these people give them a sense of false complacency. They, too, can easily fall into the trap of expecting rewards from God that equal the good works and prayers offered to him. Teresa tells these people that God does not have any need of their works. She points out that this type of giving to God, that is, giving in order to get from him, must not even be present in the imagination. The one important element God is looking for is the determination of a person's will. Catherine of Siena confirmed this point when she said: "God does not ask for a perfect work, but for infinite desire." Catherine also placed desire into prayer. She tells our pilgrims that perfect prayer is not attained through many words but through affection of desire. This desire is an intense longing to love Love in everything.

The people in these courtyards are stuck in a very pleasant rut which goes around and around in an endless circle. Everything in their lives is unchangeable and predictable. They have a set time to get up, to eat, to work, to do self-care activities, to go to the store, to go to confession, and to pray. Their prayer is routine. There is no variation in the time, place, content, or method of praying. In this way their spiritual house is kept in good order. There is no desire to change. Life is very good and comforting in its routine sameness. The element of risk is absolutely out of the question. All of life has become mesmerized in an aura of static placidity. These people shrink from a challenge as if it was a plague. They prefer that everything be safe, reliable and non-threatening.

Scattered around the third mansion are people who have a strong sense of self-righteousness. They are lifelong residents of this mansion who stand around like strong and sturdy oak trees. They consider themselves to be oracles of wisdom and lords of the manor. They are very happy because they have deluded themselves into thinking that God is happy with them. God is happy because these people are his official voice of authority on every conceivable item. These people are paragons of virtue and the bastions of the spiritual life. They are specialists on every and any religious topic and veritable fountains of spiritual knowledge. Teresa says that it is useless to give these people advice because they know all there is to know about the spiritual life. They have been peerless practitioners of virtue for so long that they can only console each other regarding who practices what virtue best. These people have a tendency to be easily shocked by the faults of others. They are more concerned about their own spiritual images than "becoming" in God's image. Everything is put into an edifying context. They are suffering for God with every little ache, every small pain, and every insignificant daily task that happens to be unpleasant. These people may be looked upon as defenders of the faith or staunch Catholics. In reality they are not giving glory to God but only giving glory to themselves. They have turned everything around in order to increase their own self-esteem. They become more attached to themselves by inappropriately padding their self-esteem through their attachment to their own wisdom and virtuous lives. They live by their own rules instead of by God's rules, for God's rules would restrict their own interpretations of the spiritual life. These people feel good by imposing their rules on others. If others do not match up, they are looked upon with disdain. These people become critical and judgmental of others because they know how devout people should act. They point their fingers at sins and do not see the brokenness of the sinners. Virtues can easily become vices here. Compassion becomes a sentimental gush. Courage turns to brashness and discernment to a critical fault-finding. Knowledge regresses to the oversimplification of spiritual doctrines. Wisdom reverts to the naive repetition of comforting cliches. Patience changes to indifference. The list is endless because every virtue has a corresponding negative quality connected to it.

Teresa tells her pilgrims that there is no cure for these permanent residents. They are, in reality, in so much misery that only compassion toward them will help. Teresa advises that no one should contradict these people for everything in their minds tells them that they are really living for God. They cannot realize that their disturbances are totally the opposite of what he is all about. It would be beneficial if these people could feel their insignificance before God. However, these residents would be totally unaware of the beauty of this enlightenment. They are so taken up with themselves that they pass the opportunity by without even noticing it. They identify very strongly with the large and sturdy oak tree. A small, insignificant acorn would not even merit a glance from them.

The oak trees are not the only trees that are found within the third mansion. As we look around we can see groups of weeping willows with their laden branches sadly swaying in the breeze. These weeping willows represent the people who are chronic complainers. They resemble the willow trees because the branches gracefully arch overhead and drop down so that the leaves are almost touching the ground. If one was standing by the trunk of this tree, one could not see past the leafy screen. These people are like the trunks of these trees and their many minor problems and small trials are represented by the leaves. How effectively the leafy branches block out hearing what others say. Their problems appear to be so great that this is their favorite topic of conversation.

In the third mansion Teresa speaks out about people who make big issues out of little events. She cautions these chronic complainers to rethink where they are in their humility. A little dryness at prayer is not a great disaster. No one should take an insignificant event, like a passing lack of devotion, and blow it all out of proportion as if it were a spiritual catastrophe. In lives that are well ordered by scheduled thoughts, words and actions, minor events that disrupt the systematized days can seem more hazardous than they really are. When people have no major problems, they tend to elaborate on the minor ones and make them sound absolutely dreadful. These people find delight in comparing illnesses from the tops of their heads to the tips of their toes. Much discussion evolves around aches, pains, diagnostic tests and various treatments. On and on they chatter about the problems of every day. Woeful problems plague them from the time they get up until the time they go to bed, and even then they do not stop. By day it is the long line at the checkout counter, the grumpy bank teller, the miseries of cleaning house, the drudgery of taking care of the yard, the traffic, the weather, the lousy service at the restaurant, the priest's long sermon last Sunday. By night it is insomnia, nightmares, cramps, letting the cat out, letting the dog in. Life is just a laborious and burdensome affair. Alas, these people are really weighed down by the garbage of incessant grumblings and gripes. They are fond of wallowing in their own miseries but think they are holy because they are living a perpetual Lent.

Proceed with reverence

Much mention is made about the fear of God by Teresa within the third mansion. The fear of God is a gift from the Holy Spirit. It confirms the virtue of hope and fills us with a great respect for the majesty of God. We do not wish to sin, lest we offend God. We also have a strong confidence in the power of his help and a deep reverence for his being. We do not fear the Lord because we are afraid of being punished or fear his anger and wrath. We fear the Lord by thinking that we may do something that is contrary to his love.

The fear of the Lord gives people a secure trust in him. Nevertheless, there are many people in the third mansion who do not fear him within the correct meaning of this phrase. They do not trust in his mercy, so they are very nervous and anxious about their own security. Teresa sees these people as poor, handwringing wretches. They cannot sleep or eat without their weapons nearby lest their enemies or robbers break into their houses and attack them or steal from them. These poor people are perpetually frightened by wondering about what may happen to them. They are constant worry warts. They appear to be tense and in a continuous state of agitation and distress. Teresa desires that these wretches ask God for help, but their apprehensions about God and his love hinder this. Their preoccupation with fear is so great it distorts their image of God. These suspicious characters are so absorbed in protecting themselves from every little harm that they neglect the wellspring of God's mercy and his care. They would do well to trust in the good God first instead of trusting in themselves. By doing this they would seek his will instead of their own. These people have a self-centered fear that prevents them from any possible progress in the spiritual life. Their reason and logic controls their actions. These two intellectual elements also develop their fear. Fear is held onto, tightly, because logical reasoning considers every frightening aspect of an event very carefully before the event takes place. Self-centered fear can take up much attention. It uncovers every area that involves risk. These people constantly worry about their image, health, family, finances, work, security, politics, prices, the weather, or any number of things. They are literally overcome by their anxieties. Worry does not help or improve anything and can tear people down. These people are much like the shrinking violets in the garden of life. Any concern of the past, present or future causes them to recoil in fear. They have not surrendered themselves or their cares to the Lord. If they did, they would know that love is a letting go of fear. To follow a way of radical love is to continually seek God's will without fear. These people will never be happy as long as they remain trapped in a state of perpetual anxiety. Authentic happiness, Teresa said, is the happiness that comes from pleasing God and seeking his will.

In the third mansion Teresa warns that there is a danger of becoming attached to things that can eventually become the ultimate end within our spiritual journey rather than a means to an end. Very good things such as wholesome acts of penance, a rule or constitutions, solitude, favorite prayers, evenings of recollection, Bible studies, religious medals, prayer groups, silence, a collection of good spiritual books, or other acts or signs of devotion are all beneficial but they are not an end in themselves. They are good practices that indicate a sincere journey in the spiritual life. If they are viewed as sacred safety belts which hold us on the path of prayer, or if they are considered as magic mysteries that would automatically open the gates of heaven, then trouble begins.

All these practices are good, if done in moderation, but they are not enough to insure a swift journey to the heart of God. Oftentimes a person can take on several devotional practices and become so wrapped up in them that they become the absolute essence of one's spirituality. Wearing a specific medal does not give one instant access to the kingdom of heaven. If a person is actively propagating the life and works of a particular saint and also engages in cutthroat tactics, blackmail or shady dealings in business or personal affairs, the saint will not come to this person's aid when the heavenly gates are reached.

It is very easy for people to get possessive of their spiritual attachments and their spiritual ways. People can also become very fond of their specific works of mercy. It is true that they are good people. Yet, in a very real way they resemble the rich, young man in the gospel of whom Teresa was so fond. The young man desired eternal life and asked Jesus how he could merit it. Jesus told him to sell all he had and give his money to the poor, then follow him. This saddened the young man for he was unwilling to give up what he had in order to gain heaven.

For those who have chosen to live in the third mansion, spiritual possessions of the permanent residents are given to God. All their good works of service are also offered. It may be hoped that all these things offered to God would cause him to grant them specific things. Do we see a spiritual bribe here? Does this kind of hope resemble a bargaining? Because these people consider themselves to be loyal servants of God and offer him all their spiritual activities, dare they think that God should immediately grant them any desired favor? Does this resemble an "I wear this, or I do this, so I get that" attitude? Teresa issues a stern warning here. She exhorts people not to ask for what they have not deserved. It should never even enter people's minds that they have merited any favors from God no matter how much they have offered or how long they have served him. Those who bargain with God and give what they think is enough have made a turn on the spiritual path that leads to nowhere. What these people are doing is giving within their own limited perspective of the word give. There is no total oblation here, only a giving of favored items.

Humility is not based on giving or on doing great deeds for God. It is grounded in seeing oneself as a useless servant. This title should rank above all other titles that a person has collected along the road of life. In this way one is less likely to put God under an obligation to grant favors according to what one has given, one's rank, one's gifts or one's accomplished works. To promote social justice, to build churches, hospitals, or schools, to heal the sick, to console, to teach, to feed the hungry, are all examples of grand and glorious ministries for God. However, it is not the specific work itself that is the main concern here. It is what a person becomes through the work that is important. If a person becomes more loving and grows in other virtues, the work has proven fruitful. Reaching the end goals of the work is secondary. What can a person really do for a God who has been so generous? No ministry could ever match his generosity to the human family. He created each person. He gave his life in order that pilgrims may be a part of his kingdom on earth and live forever in his kingdom in heaven. If true humility is present, we can only stand and gaze in awesome wonder at God's generosity. Through humility God will give us peace and conformity to see him as he really is. Humility comes as a stillness that absorbs the hurts, the hard times, the troubles and sees all in the light of the wisdom of God's will. Humility is present when there is no need for gifts and favors. The stillness of humility is like the eye of a hurricane. All forms of trouble are rampaging around, but there is a calming quiet at one's deepest center.

For those who call the third mansion home, there is a fondness for the joys, consolations and comforts of God. These people are happy and content and look for many pleasantries in prayer. They lack the perseverance that is necessary in order to carry them through the dry times that come along in prayer. They look away from the way of the cross. Although they may desire suffering, they cringe with fear when it is presented to them. When God sends them a trial, they literally jump out of their skin in fear and distress. After all, this particular type of trial was not expected.

Does the resurrection oriented spirituality that seems prevalent in the Church today contribute to the large population within the third mansion? There has been a general transition from an emphasis on dying with Jesus on the cross to rising with Christ at the resurrection. There has been a change over from self-abnegation to being totally fulfilled. There seems to be a movement from seeking God through silence, solitude, fasting and prayer, to seeking him in the service of others or in fighting for social justice.

There is no correct spirituality here. It is neither total dying nor total rising. A healthy blending of the components of both of these schools of spirituality would be ideal. We can only appreciate the resurrection if we have gone through adversity. If Jesus' death and resurrection are well balanced within our lives, they will flow into the sorrows and joys of our journeys of life and enrich them.

In these days, though, it seems as if the scales are tipped toward emphasis on the resurrection. We must watch in order not to fall into an extreme position here. An indication of this may be that certain eucharistic celebrations may be over celebrated with music and song that resemble a spectacular performance. We may become totally involved with activities that assist others in one way or another and disregard our prayer life. This, if it goes on nonstop, can quickly lead to burn-out. We cannot cure all the ills of the world by repeating an occasional alleluia while feverishly racing from one activity to another all day long. It is possible that all good work may be done in the name of the risen Christ, but if we do not take time out to pray each day, we are lost.

Neither can we pray and think about the cross all day. Other activities are needed for a sound psychological balance. Common sense and self-discipline will take us along the right road. Suffering will always be shrouded in mystery and can never be understood with our finite minds. Some of us may take great lengths to avoid suffering. When we do not accept it gracefully, we are arresting our own development as total persons. The grain of wheat died before it could bear fruit. So did Jesus. By accepting suffering in a grace-filled manner, so can we.

Teresa cites a few examples that illustrate the need for letting go in order to make advancement in the third mansion. Both incidents indicate difficulty in conforming to the grace that comes through change.

There once was a wealthy gentleman who had no wife, no children, nor anyone else who was dependent on him for their needs. He truly enjoyed the pleasures of luxurious living. When a recession came into being, this man suddenly found himself reduced to the social level called middle class. To be more specific, it was upper middle class. He still maintained a moderately large savings account and also had set up several retirement funds. He still attended social functions and cultural events as was his custom. He was living quite comfortably and was enjoying good financial security, but it was not at the high level that was his usual fashion. Our gentleman was in a constant state of worry and distress. He worried as if he did not have one bit of food left in the house to eat. He justified his anxiety by repeating to himself that if his wealth were returned, he would surely use it to feed the poor children. The man really had nothing to worry about. Because of his anxiety, he was experiencing great difficulty finding God in his new living situation. Instead of being satisfied with his lot and doing the best he could with what he had, this man was fighting God's plan with his own wishes. His incessant desire to have things the way they were and his current inordinate anxiety, that was ungrounded, were like walls that prevented a receptivity to God's continuing plans from becoming known to him. He will have trouble finding inner peace as long as he is fixated on his own desires and distress.

A similar event takes place when there is a change in a person's status or position. The change could be in the form of a step down or alteration within the areas of social, marital or vocational status. This may occur when an individual changes jobs. A job may be found closer to home, but it is a lower position than in one's previous employment. There could be a move in a person's company or religious congregation, to a job that has less prestige. One's job may have been eliminated due to budget cuts. Shifts could also come about through change in marital status, transition from one religious community to another, leaving the religious life, retirement, accident or illness. During the spiritual journey, good people have often reflected on how Jesus suffered and the positive aspects that come through suffering. They may have thought that they would like to experience something similar so they could be more like Jesus. Now it has happened to them, but it has taken a form which was least expected. A form of suffering is theirs, but they find that it is not as easy as it seemed to be. Their well-ordered lives are shattered. They are facing feelings and emotions they were previously unaware of because everything was so regulated in their lives. How will they cope? Do these people rule their emotions, or will their emotions rule them? If it is the latter, the people, seemingly, will have difficulty in adjusting their wills to God's plan. Humility is the ointment for any wound, be it economic, physical, psychological, social or spiritual. In times of trial we really find out the meaning of the phrase: "When God closes a door he opens a window." With patience, we must look for this window. We will not find it if we simply withdraw into a state of inertia.

The key factor that indicates if our pilgrims are to stay in one of the many lifetime residences of the third mansion or progress through it is the absence or presence of humility. If humility is absent, the pilgrims know well what will happen. If humility is present, this mansion is one of continuous growth. Our pilgrims recognize the comforts and distractions of life, adapt to them, and then let them go. Through this ongoing process God can give freely to the pilgrims, and he does give in a much greater way than any of the homesteaders in the third mansion have experienced. Humility brings great solace. After unfavorable events have been put into their proper perspective, human beings experience this solace from God. Afterwards they can only respond with loving gratitude toward God. There is no desire to ask for spiritual consolations, for these are not the elements that lead to the pursuit of perfection.

How can our pilgrims evaluate themselves to see where they stand on the scale of humility? Perhaps these questions may help. Do they feel shattered when slighted in small ways? Is their dignity diminished when someone else gets his or her way? Do they feel put out because they have been passed over for a high position that was just vacated? Do they continually compare themselves with others? Do they feel unappreciated, unloved, unwanted or uncared for over long periods of time? Do they conceal their negative reactions by putting on pious airs and wearing a sweet smile? Do they continually feel cornered, worthless, walked on, used, laughed at or excluded? There are many other questions that would fit in this area. The major question regarding the virtue of humility could well be: Do our pilgrims seek God in all things? It would be profitable for our pilgrims to make a list of how they find God in all things. The more they find God, the more they will be able to respond with love, and in the end love is all that matters. Love given, in all its radicalism and in all its wildness, brings our pilgrims along the path to God. If they are determined to love without measure, that love can be generously given. It will not only be given to God, it will spread to others. Love's warmth is contagious. It will spread like the flames that can be lit from the light of one candle.

More about the residents

The people who have chosen to dwell in the third mansion are like walnuts. The fruit of this nut represents the self. These people are good people, but they are so bundled up within themselves that they will never crack through their shells and branch out into the open. The fruit of the walnut has many convolutions. All these wrinkles and crevices offer an unlimited opportunity for endless explorations to be made inside the shell. So, too are these people. They are caught up in their own ways of looking at things and dealing with them. They are very much tied up in their own routines. By being so engrossed with themselves, they become enclosed within themselves. The outer shells protect them from outside influences. As long as the shell is not cracked open there is no opportunity for growth. There is no way to reach God, nor is there any way to open oneself up to his love. These people seem stubborn and unyielding.

There comes to mind a story: Once upon a time there was a contemplative monastery filled with very good monks. The monastery enjoyed an admirable reputation and the monks were revered as holy men of God. There was one extraordinary brother among the monks who knew and loved sacred scripture very much. In fact, he was a noted scripture scholar. He knew the Bible so well and so thoroughly that he always answered every question he was asked by quoting from the Bible. The time passed by, and soon the good brethren became irritated by the way our Bible brother responded to questions. In a short while the irritation grew, and the good brethren were sure they were going crazy. It seemed as if there was a full-fledged epidemic of monastic madness going on inside each monk. There were murmurings of frequent headaches, stomach aches, and heated whisperings among the monks. To the outsider everything seemed quite serene. The abbot, who was well known for his saintly ways, decided to put a stop to this. He greatly desired to save the mortal bodies and immortal souls of these desperate monks. He knew what the trouble was, for there had been frequent knockings at his door. He called our Bible brother into his office and said to him, "From this day forward, under holy obedience, I forbid you to answer a question by quoting from scripture."

Our Bible brother smiled, bowed, and did what he was told without question. A few months had passed, and one day the good brother cook found a jackass in the refectory. He tried to lead it out but to no avail. The other monks tried without success. Each monk tried alone, then they banded together. They had exhausted all possible ideas. The jackass remained in the refectory. This caused quite a quandary. The abbot could not contain himself. He found our Bible brother and said, "I lift your obedience from you this one time. Please describe for me, through scripture, the problem that is now in our refectory." Our brother smiled, and said without hesitation, "He came unto his own and his own received him not."

Cheers to the jackass in all of us! It is by recognizing him that our pilgrims do not tarry in the warm and comforting chambers of the third mansion. The sophisticated and stoic sentinels that patrol the permanent dwellings do not appreciate pilgrims who can laugh at themselves and love God with a hearty abandonment. They frown upon anyone who creates any forms of chaos that challenge.

As we look up and down the long and broad corridors that stretch themselves in labyrinthine fashion throughout the areas for permanent residents within the third mansion, we can see a vast number of pedestals. Fortunately, a large number of these pedestals have been vacated since Vatican II. Oh, but we notice that there are still a small number that are occupied. The people who live on these pedestals stepped up on them when they entered the seminary, religious life, or other positions in religion and never bothered to step down. It may be in the realm of possibility that these pedestal dwellers entered religion to seek an identity which gave more stability and security than their pre-entrance identity gave. These people may consider themselves as clothed in an exclusiveness that places them above others. Oh, they are good clergy and good religious people. Their pedestal status is reinforced by adoring laity. They maintain their image by being and doing everything that an exemplary religious person is supposed to do. They are ideal for the public and work tirelessly in their apostolates. They are admired and esteemed. They maintain a proper reserve when speaking with non-religious persons. They have no long-term, meaningful relationships. They are so busy doing the work of God that they do not have the time for such things. However, they may tremble when they are not addressed by their appropriate titles. They may moan when they are not shown the proper signs of respect. Ah, and the people they live with, plus observant others, notice that there is trouble. There may be a few anomalous character defects that need to be recognized and healed. Often these defects may not be observable either by others or by the person who has them. Nonetheless, noticeable symptoms may be present. Alcoholism, drug dependency, workaholism, subservient actions toward, and/or inappropriate remarks about the opposite sex, continuous abusive language, and other repeated aberrations are sound external signs which show that all is not well internally. Authentic service to others develops when there is a peacefulness that comes from one's inner world. The competent, care-giving religious person is authentic when there is a stable, unique, mature personal identity that functions in the spectrums of wellness and personal integration. A person with inner peace and integration serves others with a life-giving energy that expresses itself through gestures of goodness, tenderness, truth, respect and reverence.

There are some active religious who may be hindered in their progress through the third mansion. The block comes from a need to be a highly respected business or professional person. This need supersedes the desire to be a faith-filled religious. Religious who are continually striving for professional excellence may be neglecting their spiritual development. If this is happening, it can evolve into spiritual apathy. There may be a superficial integration within the professionally competent religious whose spirituality lies in a mediocre state. What are the signs that may indicate if a religious is over extended in the professional or business realm of his or her life? Here are some inquiries that may shed some light on this subject. The religious may want to ask himself or herself the following questions: What are the professional and spiritual priorities in my life? Are they balanced well, or does one greatly outweigh the other? How many professionally related continuing educational opportunities did I attend during the past year? How many spiritual enriching opportunities did I attend during the past year? When I talk to God in prayer, does my language resemble the same language patterns I use when I talk to business and professional associates? Does it resemble speaking patterns I use when I talk to students, patients or clients? Am I so involved in my work that I can only make excuses not to attend an extended retreat, desert experience or other long-term spiritual activity that involves personal spiritual direction? Does the thought of a day or two with nothing to do frighten me to a frenzy? Do I feel good because I draw a high salary? How much of my reading is devoted to my work, and how much is devoted to my spiritual development? Have I developed a pompous attitude about my professional status?

An important aspect to consider when responding to these questions is honesty. One can cheat others, one can cheat one's supervisors and superiors, one can cheat one's self, but one cannot cheat God. The purpose of religious life is not based on being a thriving success in one's profession but rather in being faithful to the call of Jesus and living the gospels. By living the message of Jesus, religious and all Christians are responding to the call of holiness.

Specific religious communities may appear in the pavilions of the third mansion. If all religious communities were placed side by side along a continuum, houses that may be located in the third mansion are at the polarity groups that form the beginning and the end of this continuum. If we were to visit these houses, we would find two quite different expressions of religious life. Many of the components that make up these expressions might have difficulty in blending well to form a viable, functional, authentic expression of religious life.

On the reserved right of this spectrum we find a very strict expression of religious life. Here everyone is totally dependent on the superior for everything. There may be a parent/child interaction here. The holy rule is absolute law. The members of these communities have no say in what they would like to do. The daily events are in common, performed on a set time schedule. The absentees often feel guilty when they cannot participate in community activities. Community life is number one at all times and in all places. Everyone knows where everyone else is and what they are doing. Everything is geared toward building the community spirit and its apostolates. Contact with outsiders is discouraged. Community members lead a protective, sheltered, structured life style. All troubles or conflicts between community members are taken to the superior. Relationships between community members are polite, cordial, and courteous. No one rocks the boat. No one stirs things up. There is very little time for privacy and personal activities. There is not much variety or creativity during the passing days. No member dares mention change because things have always been done that way. Early on in their formation, members are taught what to pray, when to pray, where to pray, and how to pray.

On the liberal left we find a very loose expression of religious life. These communities resemble boarding houses or middle class hotels where members come and go at will. The interactions within the community are superficial. There is minimal or no exchange of feelings, desires, goals or anything else that lies deep in the heart. No community spirit or identity is evident and there is little sense of belonging. The rules are made by individual members and usually directed toward the self-fulfillment of these members. There is much television watching in the evenings. On weekends or holidays the house is empty, the community members are scattered to the four winds. The members are easy prey to current fads, fashions and trivia. They have the latest in sports equipment, and participate in the newest recreational activities. They attend contemporary movies, plays and concerts often. Community life very much resembles fraternity or sorority living. Frequently members invite friends in without considering the need for privacy of the other community members. The members of these communities pray when they want, if they want, and where they want. No set prayer schedule is followed. Many members believe that everything is a prayer.

Doing acts of penance is very popular within the spiritual activities of the third mansion. The people practice penance as they practice everything else in their lives. They are very much in control of what they do. They practice visual expressions of penance so everyone else will know what they are doing. Yet they are very careful, as they do not want to take any chances in ruining their very good physiques.

During the days prior to Vatican II, people were very aware of what their neighbors were doing. Strict adherence to regulations regarding Friday abstinence, Lenten fastings and the penitential preparations of Advent separated the good Catholics from the backsliders. These external customs were practiced with great fervor. There were endless discussions on who was giving up what for Lent, and eating meat on Friday was an unspeakable sin.

Giving up something for Lent is still common today. Let us look at a resident of the third mansion and see what his Lenten specialty is. As we amble around the dimly lit hallways in the evening, we can easily spot our example. There he is, sitting at the same place he sits every night, eyes glued to the television. He watches the same round of programs day after day, week after week. He would rather watch TV than do anything else, but when Lent comes around each year he makes his one big sacrifice. The TV is shut off for forty long days and forty longer nights. He frets and moans during the long lonesome Lenten evenings. All his family and friends know about his great sacrifice. Despite his distress, he passes through Lent with flying colors. Not once did he turn on the TV. It was not easy. It was about the hardest thing he ever did. He almost cried when he missed the baseball games and other weekend sports events. Oh, what an agony! He was offering it all up, and everyone was aware of this.

Here is the perfect example of the trap of penance that can tie a person up and securely hold him or her in the third mansion for life. This penitential practice is brimming with pride. Penance should lead to a greater need of God's mercy in one's life. In this case the person who gave up TV heartily congratulated himself for a job well done. He was reinforced in his supreme sacrifice by sympathizing family and friends. He gratified himself by his incessant groanings. He was in no way acknowledging his weaknesses before God and dependence on his compassion.

The Vatican Council has asked us to look more deeply into our lives and seek to discover the need for the type of penance that would draw us quietly into a deeper realization of the mystery of the cross. We should strive to see how this mystery is revealed in our own lives. In order to be true seekers of God we must be forgiving people. This is more difficult than the external forms of penance because it requires an internal letting go. It is not easy to rid ourselves of long-term feuds, inveterate feelings of resentment, revenge or anger, or petty bickering. Abstaining from having the last word in an argument, giving excuses, avoiding defenses so commonly spoken when we feel the least bit threatened, or forgetting the insults we have received also comes into focus here. There are many menacing nuisances we can place on our junk piles. Persistent arguing, backbiting, criticizing, temper tantrums, spiteful words, little ways of calling attention to how good we are, getting even, all have a place, not in our hearts, but on our little piles of junk that should be discarded. All these vexing items, after they are uprooted, should be kept out. A herculean task, but we might think of others who may have been hurt by them. We can really understand God's forgiving mercy when we face these negative traits eyeball to eyeball. By facing our own shortcomings, we become more forgiving of the faults and foibles of others.

Penance does not mean doing something that makes us feel good spiritually. If we do penance to feel good, it is as if we are saying we love God, but the love is only partial. It is not a wholehearted giving. There is a protection of self through doing penance because it is only done for self-gratification. Again, there is a giving within penance, but the giving is limited to how much the self wants to give. It only goes to the "feeling good" stage. In doing our own penances in our own way, we strengthen, in a false way, our self-esteem. We rationalize that this is living for God. It is a living for God with a "me first" mentality.

A generous person takes forgiveness in stride. There are no grudges to hold. He or she pardons easily and is always looking for ways to please God. One takes risks for him. This cannot be done if the individual is caught in the mire of disagreeable incidents that happened in the past. It cannot be done in a patterned, well-ordered life where everything is predictable. Generosity is based in every encounter with others, in the task at the present moment, in disappointments, in joys, in humiliations, and in all other events of the days. The generous person meets everything that comes along in life with a resilient stride. There is no waiting for the great test from the Lord where a person can prove his or her generosity, because there is a day by day acceptance of life. Generosity is found each moment in which one seeks to serve and each moment in which one is faithful to one's duties. It is giving beyond measure. Generosity is a cheerful acceptance of the tedious, the humdrum, the empty, the frustrating, the boring, the menial, the intimidating, the unromantic and the unrewarding events of life.

Those penitents who think they are doing great things for God by their great mortifications and great sufferings are in for a rude awakening. No amount of suffering and sacrifice can bring God to these people. He gives to those who are humble, to those who know they have earned nothing, and to those who love him as Father and rely on his mercy. A prideful, over-inflated ego can never make a person ready for God, and a prideful ego can be found in the strangest places! It may be found in one's vocation, service to others, spiritual practices or even intellect.

The third mansion can be called the great divider, for it separates our pilgrims into two groups. There are the settlers and the pioneers. The settlers have become quite at home here and have decided to take up their abode somewhere in the peaceful, quiet rooms where nothing much is required of them, and everything is cut and dried. All necessary questions are answered. All records are up to date. Everything is easily definable. There is a distinct difference between right and wrong, good and bad, yes and no, white and black, beautiful and ugly. There is law and order, and best of all, stability and security. God is the sheriff. He is more feared than loved by the settlers. They shake in their boots lest they break the law and then must be punished. Sometimes there is a preoccupation with the minutiae of the law. God, the sheriff, governs by rules and regulations. Everything is always on schedule and runs perfectly. Bake sales, boutiques, pot luck dinners, religious education meetings, parish festivals all run without a hitch. Emily Post would be proud. The settlers fear anything or anyone that comes from outside of this mansion. They also fear venturing into higher mansions. Their motto is safety first, always. Their main concern is to stay in the good graces of the sheriff. Settlers are generous in their weekly church contributions. After all, in the end, at the last round-up, a big account in the heavenly bank will be beneficial in getting through those pearly gates.

The second group of pilgrims are the pioneers. Their religion is based on their ability to love. They are smaller in number than the first group, but they have more guts than the entire static population within the lower mansions. The pioneers are the doers, the innovators, the risk takers, the go getters, the people with an untameable wildness about them. They depend on God to lead them through the many gray areas of life. The pioneers see life as an ongoing adventure. They enjoy talking about the myriad aspects of God and his love. Pioneers are always on the move exploring his vast creations. There is no place that is called home. Pioneers do not glory in their achievements nor become stuck in the mud. God is a full of life companion on the journey called life. He is real, daring, personal and rugged. Without God in their lives, the pioneers would become lazy and would not move. The pioneers are hungry for adventure with God. They take chances. They are daring. They thrive on challenges. They work hard, live hard, play hard, and pray hard. Faith has the spirit of adventure that lies in readiness to move on. It is the joy of another day that is made to push into the unknown. Life is a journey based on deepening the pioneer's capacity to love and be loved.

Time for reflection

Our sincere pilgrims are aware of the dangers that lie in the third mansion. They desire progression to the higher mansions, yet seem fixated in their present location because they do not know, precisely, what to do. They do not want this fixation to be permanent, yet they lack the intuition that is needed to focus on the problem areas in themselves. What can they do? They see trouble spots in others but, as yet, our pilgrims cannot identify with these spots in a personal way because they remain hidden from their conscious minds. What can be done in order to become aware of the stumbling blocks that lie unnoticed or unrecognized?

If one places oneself, openly and honestly, in the loving presence of God, then admits to God and to self that there are, indeed, problem areas to be discovered and overcome, the first step already has been taken. To realize that problems are present, even if they have not been specifically defined, is a big step forward. It is the self admitting that there needs to be work done inside. Improvements are to be made in the old ego if the spiritual journey is to continue. It is an admission that an individual does not know all, and that he or she is willing to seek and learn. It is a reliance on God. It is a trusting in others.

There are several paths our pilgrims could take in order to receive assistance in identifying and defining the problem areas within. Counsel from a well-qualified spiritual director may prove to be very beneficial. It is very important that a person has confidence in the spiritual director and that he or she can express himself or herself freely and honestly to this person. The spiritual director should be a person of prayer and have a sound knowledge of theology and the social and behavioral sciences.

Another source is well known to all. It is called an examination of conscience. The examination that is proposed here is a bit different from the ones with which our readers may be familiar. These questions would fit under the heading of an introspective self-evaluation very well. They require courage and an ultimate honesty with self. The answers will take time. If one so chooses, one may wish to record one's initial thoughts, then review the questions and answer them again in the weeks or months ahead. An interesting comparative study may result. The answers to these questions are subjective to each person responding. An individual should note that authentic self-examination is painful. Concerning the unfavorable answers that arise, it would be beneficial to spend some time probing into the reasons behind them.

- What do I value?
- What are my short- and long-term goals?
- Are they realistic and genuine or just for show?
- How do my decisions and goals express my values?
- Am I able to postpone gratification and pass up immediate pleasure or profit for a long-term goal?
- What are my personal priorities?
- How well do my daily activities reflect my priorities?
- How do I use my time and energy in responding to my priorities?
- Am I able to make a decision, act on it, and be responsible for its outcome?
- Am I able to work on a project or activity in spite of opposition and discouraging setbacks?
- Am I able to accept responsibility for my own attitudes, feelings, failures, and prejudices, or do I have a tendency to project or displace my attitudes or feelings on other persons or things?
- Am I able to acknowledge my own anger, bias and limitations to myself and to others?
- How well do I express my anger with God?
- Am I able to handle frustrations and settle differences without violence or destruction?
- Am I able to recognize, accept and articulate disappointments, unpleasantries and losses, and feel the pain and anguish they cause?
- Am I able to remain calm in the midst of chaos?
- Can I disagree without being disagreeable?
- Am I able to say "I am sorry" or "I was wrong" easily, and if proven right refrain from saying "I told you so"?
- How often do I admit that I do not have all the answers?
- Do I have a tendency to have the last word in a disagreement?
- When I feel a negative response that may hurt arise from within, am I able to stop it before it is verbalized?

- How do I accept constructive criticism and compliments?
- How do I refrain from using my self-defeating, self-limiting defense mechanisms?
- How often do I keep my word?
- How often do I make excuses?
- How often do I think of doing a good action or work, then neglect or refuse to do it?
- Am I chronically tardy?
- How often do I put work and other tasks ahead of people?
- How well am I in touch with, and how do I express my positive feelings?
- How do I love myself as a God created, unique person of worth?
- How am I open to God's leadings in the daily events and decisions of my life?
- How do I consider what he might want of me?
- Am I able to, and if so how do I, live in peace with things I cannot change?
- How do I give and receive emotional support?
- Do I find more satisfaction in receiving than in giving?
- How do I sincerely care for others and respond to their needs?
- To what degree do I accept others as they are and where they are?
- What is the consistency and quality of my human relationship?

The answers to the above questions are not easy, and no one is expected to have a perfect score. These questions give a person an understanding of the elements that, at present, contribute to his or her orientation. Each response reflects what kind of person an individual is. Was there a strong defense of current behaviors? Was there a look at one's behaviors as Jesus might have seen them? Was there a significant amount of time spent investigating the motives behind a yes, no, or short answer? There is never-ending work regarding self-knowledge. The more a person grows in self-knowledge, the more he or she will grow in the knowledge of God.

It is known that in the third mansion we can easily become creatures of habit. Habitual behavior plugs right into predictability and predictability is a trademark often observed here. This can be illustrated by our television addict presented earlier. His continued TV watching is not an edifying trait. He may alter this behavior by applying a specific set of questions that are directed to this particular activity. Perhaps he can find a more practical guide for his viewing habits. We wonder how he would respond to the following inquiries:

- How much time does he spend watching TV each day?
- How much time does he spend in prayer each day?
- What are the reasons he watches TV? (Could they be to find out what is happening in the world or other positive reasons, or are there negative reasons such as killing time, seeking an avoidance of work, or an avoidance of communicating with others?)
- Does he watch quality programs (educational, recreational, historical or cultural), or does he watch a monotonous continuation of game shows, situation comedies, or movie re-runs?
- Is the TV on when no one is in the room watching it?
- Does this man hog the tube when watching it with others, demanding to see his own favorite programs without any thought of what the others would like?
- How high is the TV on his list of priorities, values, and goals?
- Is there an incessant need to watch the news repeatedly each day?
- Is there an addiction to programs that are rude, crude, violent, offensive, insulting, demeaning or otherwise inappropriate?

Sincere answers to these questions will tell this man if he is addicted to his TV, or if the TV is prioritized within its proper place in his life style.

There is yet another option that may be considered for possible problem identification. This option can only be helpful after the self-evaluation has been made, and needs two prerequisites in order for it to be effective. First, the person must be open. This means that there is a readiness to seek and accept help. Second, the person must have a workable skill in the art of listening. This means listening with the mouth closed.

Openness lifts us from the darkness of our own making. Darkness stems from the loneliness of a self that is centered upon self. It is through being open that the release from self is made. When we are genuinely open, we see God in others. Thomas Merton stated this in a beautiful way: "His one image is in us all," he said, "and we discover him by discovering the likeness of his image in one another."

Listening involves the silence of self and a hearing from the heart. It is paying careful and undivided attention to the other in order to deeply understand. When we understand from the heart, we are genuinely touched by the other.

When one has a working knowledge of these two traits, one may wish to talk to a good friend regarding one's self-made stumbling blocks that have brought one's spiritual journey to a screeching halt. Often a close friend may see traits about a person's self that the self refuses to see. The refusal may come through lack of insight, self-defeating defense mechanisms of which an individual is unaware, hidden wounds, self-made walls, or any other medium that shields the self from hurt.

Before we proceed further, we would like to confirm the distinction between good friends and acquaintances. It is with the former that long-standing relationships are built. The latter pass in and out of a person's life in a rather rapid and regular fashion. Acquaintances can brighten the days by a smile or pleasant remark, or they may darken the days in minor ways. Whatever their influence, they are chance contacts that leave no deeply significant mark on one's existence. During these brief encounters, acquaintances deserve a person's loving presence and attention. However, since these meetings resemble passing ships in the night, they were not meant to be developed into anything more than what they are.

Within the third mansion Teresa, again, places her strong seal of approval on good friends. She tells our pilgrims that these friends would be advisable to consult so that her pilgrims do not become self-centered in anything. She also states that it would be beneficial if these good friends were mature and wise. She knows well that true friendships are a gift from God. Ecclesiastics 6:14 reveals that: "A faithful friend is a true shelter, whoever finds one has found a rare treasure. A faithful friend is something beyond price. There is no measuring his worth." Teresa was richly gifted by many "treasures" in her life.

Good friends are not easily acquired. They can never be bought, for love cannot be bought. Friendship is a priceless gift that is freely given and freely accepted. It is a gift that develops and grows as the years pass. It matures through an ever deepening commitment. It is a sharing of strengths and weaknesses and a growing that comes through a mutual give and take. A human being's ability to love is possible because he or she was created in the image and likeness of a God who is love. Good friends experience this love and what it means to personally give and receive this love. Friendships that are rich and deep are also demanding. The demands of time and energy are not negative in any way for there is loyalty to one another and a freedom from any selfish desires. Good friendships are like adventures. They involve personal risk but are well worth these risks. Risks are very necessary for such a journey. There will be troubles and difficulties along the way, but these, too, are needed if the friendship is to grow. The ways in which we are able to love, and the measure by which we give and receive love in this world, will be a reflection of how well we will be able to love in the next.

Intimate friends are rare, for they are grounded in self-forgetfulness. The generous person who knows how to love others is richer than the greedy person who seeks to control others. The person who knows love is not afraid to lose anything for all is given freely. The person who can manipulate and control others cannot hold on to anything with comfort, because there are just too many possessions of which to keep track.

Since the love one holds for an intimate friend comes from God's love and is a sign to all of his love, the love one has for the friend is reflected to all one's acquaintances. A sensitivity to others is acquired when an individual deeply shares both the positive and negative aspects of his or her life with a heart friend. Joys and sorrows, successes and failures, pleasantries and pain, dreams and frustrations, consolations and conflicts all take on a deeper meaning when shared with a person who truly understands. In listening to a heart friend, one refines one's skills in being attentive to others who pass through one's life. Attentive listening develops a simple expression of concern to another whom, most likely, a person would never see again. This concern is a very powerful witness to the God of love.

In the third mansion a pilgrim usually finds a good friend. The attraction first felt in the second mansion leads to a type of commitment. This commitment involves time and energy that is spent with the friend. There is a sharing beyond the superficial or mundane, a mutual enjoyment, and a pleasure that comes in doing for and being with the other. The danger here, as in the danger in prayer, is that the person wants to do what he or she wants to do and give what he or she wants to give. There is still a strong element of self here. The blessings of intimate friendships are just beginning to be experienced in this mansion. Some pilgrims will grow in their friendships faster than others. If one feels comfortable with this new friendship and secure in it, one may consider learning more about one's self through this friend.

If talking with the good friend is to be fruitful, two areas must be avoided like the plague. The purpose for such a meeting is a deep evaluation of self. This meeting could prove disastrous if an emphasis was placed totally on a person's weaknesses. To continually dwell on one's newly found negative traits would leave one feeling flat as a pancake. It would be as if an individual had been run over by a steam roller. This would result in a poor self-image which is no good for anyone. A healthy balance can be reached by identifying one's possible faults and failings and also reaffirming one's gifts and talents. There even may be a discovery of some new talents here! This gives a human being a blending of weaknesses and strengths which every person possesses. Absolutely no individual is either total weakness or total strength.

A meeting such as this may begin well, and be rich with good intentions, but since the intimate friendship is so new, a person may fall away from this purpose and intention soon after the meeting has started. If the meeting takes a negative turn, it would prove harmful to both parties. One's frail humanness often needs support, but support must be of the beneficial type. Inappropriate support becomes present when two people band together to confirm and reconfirm false ways of thinking. This is reinforced by mutual criticism of specific others, gaining strength through citing the poor behavior of specific others or attacking and tearing them down in order to build up self. A person may also recite the faults of others to justify his or her own faults. There are other easy pitfalls. Cynicism, negative gossiping, tale bearing, trivializing, self pity, martyrism or defeatist characteristics can be very easy traps to fall into. An individual may avoid these common potholes along the road of quality friendships by making a real effort to see and speak of the good qualities of others. In this way one can build up others rather than tear them down.

Our ability to relate to God, our ability to relate to others, and our ability to maintain sincere, mature, long-term friendships depend heavily on how we relate to ourselves. Our relationships with significant others mirror our relationship with ourselves and our relationship with God. How well we deal with others depends on our own level of maturity. Blessed is the person who has an intimate friend.

Many times flashes of insight that increase our self-knowledge come from good friends. Often these insights can leave us changed persons. Such moments come to us all, but they are not limited to coming from friends. They can be found in a sermon, a line of poetry, a potent quote, a fairy tale, a seminar, a summer's vacation, a short story, or even a stroll along the seashore. There is really no limit to where we may find insightful and inspirational words. Where is really not a challenge. The challenge is if the individual seeking insights is able to recognize the potential worth of the quote, assimilate it into his or her heart, integrate it into his or her being, and use it in a beneficial way. This means putting it into practice internally and being able to share it, meaningfully, with others.

If our pilgrims are to go beyond the third mansion, there must be the desire to give up the feeling of being the good Christian, the holy person, or the wonderful or nice individual. There must be a letting go of the need to be an inspirational, admired, or respected spiritual person. An indifference as to what kinds of virtues our pilgrims have is also required. This is the beginning of purgation, of purification. The pilgrims in this mansion must have the ability to risk if they expect to grow. They risk an openness which allows God to be God and lets the good friend be the good friend in their lives. Risk will involve pain. The risk of pain increases as the pilgrims grow in love. This urges love to lead them onward into a mystery that is not understood and allows for the first real expressions of spiritual vulnerability, sensitivity and spontaneity to be present. It is then that prayer changes from an intellectual mode to one of simplicity that comes through the gentle workings of God's Spirit in the soft stirrings of the heart.

By traveling through the third mansion and by successfully coming to the entrance of the fourth mansion, our pilgrims have found that there was a strong affirmation in love as being a choice. Something new was also learned. This choice, in order to fully reflect love, must be the decision that requires the greater good and the most courage. Today we can easily imagine Teresa standing at the door of the fourth mansion. She is urging her hearty pilgrims forward telling them that they have now sincerely and seriously given themselves to a life of true prayer. In doing this, they have opened themselves fully to God's actions within their lives. She exhorts them to go forward as strong women and men and follow in the footsteps of Mary, our leader in the pilgrimage of faith. In hearing this the pilgrims become more awed at the mother of God and more appreciative of her influence in their lives. She, as perfect model, has lit the way ahead by her passage along that mysterious road many years ago. Now it is dark, but the pilgrims remember that the way ahead was an unknown way for Mary also. Our pilgrims desire a light in order to tread safely, but there are no lamps outside, only the warm light within. Mary, too, had no directions to point the way. Our pilgrims feel a deep kinship with her as the journey ahead will be through strange and unpopulated chambers. The pilgrims can only walk forward bravely, as Mary did, keeping their hands firmly in the hand of God.

Fourth Mansion

A PLACE OF TRANSITION

Our fourth mansion may be seen as an expensive bridge that connects the human with the divine. It is a place of transition. Faith resembles a leap in the dark. Prayer takes on a new dimension. The supernatural element of the spiritual life is initially experienced. Our pilgrims feel as if they are jumping off an Alpine cliff here. They do not know where they are going to land, but their trust in God tells them that they will land somewhere.

This mansion may, at first, give our pilgrims an uneasy feeling. Mysticism, and any other synonyms connected with this word, are shrouded with sinister, suspicious mystery that oscillates around the occult. Are mystics or mystical elements that flow from God really that mysterious? It hardly seems so. One's next door neighbor may even be one. The only element that separates the person who seems to have a mystical orientation—and this means a healthy mystical orientation—from ordinary folks is that the person labeled mystic sees the common events of each day as small miracles gifted from God. A mystical quality develops from a nature that is steeped in contemplation. The gift of contemplation is given to a person by God, perhaps as a seed planted deep in the heart. The person slowly discovers this seed, tends to its growth with help from God's quiet graces, and rests in this aspect of his or her being. It is only after a person has walked along the path of the spiritual life for some time that the gift of contemplation becomes God centered. There are more true contemplatives walking on the roads of the world than there are behind monastic walls. All are pilgrims of faith and their ability to ponder things deeply gives them the grace to see God in the good, the bad and the ugly. To be able to see God in the refuse invokes a sense of mystery that goes beyond rational cognition. Yes, the mystics are filled with awe and wonder as they gaze upon the manifold expressions of God. Yet, their feet are planted firmly on the ground. Individuals who experience God at such depths are thoroughly imbued with wholesome attitudes, sound personality traits and practical, down to earth realism.

If one has met people considered to be mystics, one has seen calm, prayerful people who are open minded, alert, level headed, and possessive of an irrepressible sense of humor. Common sense reigns supreme among their attributes. Mystical people can be found, most likely, seeking the Lord among the pots and pans in the kitchen or the leaves and lawn of the backyard. A person is least likely to find them spending hours and hours on their knees in the chapel. Their mouths do not utter a continuum of pious phrases or holy mutterings, nor do they have any other mannerisms or speech patterns that feed into an airy fairy frame of reference. Mystical people are very real, genuine human types who can share in laughter and grief and are at their best when relating a jovial jocularity, or sharing their favorite recipe, or discussing the latest discovery in space technology. They may even know the best way to photograph still life.

In this mansion our pilgrims find that their active prayer is gradually becoming graced by passive prayer. There is a change from thinking about God, to being for God. The human effort that is channeled into prayer decreases as the divine indwelling slowly begins to emerge and is experienced as God coming from one's core. Henceforth, the individual will experience less and less of self within and more and more of God within. This mansion marks the beginning of the supernatural or mystical experience, because our pilgrims have moved closer to the King of Glory. The rooms in this mansion are beautiful. The beauty is so delicate and so fragile that the pilgrims, through their intellect, cannot explain or comprehend it.

The fourth mansion can be perplexing and confusing simply because the unknown is experienced in a way which defies understanding. It is a mansion that requires a faith that is based on complete confidence in God. There are no external props to support our pilgrims. Faith is not derived from the rational lights of reason, comforts from good feelings, or the intellectual processes which indicate that a God must exist. It is a simple, bare bones, trusting in divine providence.

Our society, which is so rooted in the scientific method for problem solving, computers, and advanced technology, opposes what the fourth mansion has to offer. The type of faith that is found in the fourth mansion could leave our pilgrims who relate from a head orientation, that is, using a high cerebral perspective, very nervous indeed. These pilgrims have assiduously sought after God through scholarly and academic pursuits. Knowledge of him has been their primary mental activity. They have based their faith on relating the known to the unknown. They then assimilate the unknown, because it has become familiar through experi-

Gelcaps (100 + 50 FREE) or
120 ct. Liquigel or Migraine
Caplets, Caplets or
(80 + 40 FREE)

6 99

Official
LPGA
Event

SCN AB

Page For Sale Effective Dates

Caplets

verberating circuits of their cell assemblies which
ocortex of their brains. After an understanding has
plunge further into the unknown through a more
knowledge of God was found through research and
ourses, workshops and lectures, and reviewing reams
er data that were collected from the many facets of

the first three mansions information has been gathered,
d integrated into their minds. Much knowledge has been
t God and the spiritual journey. This has been good and has
firm foundation on which to build. Faith was discovered,
nd formulated through diligent study and a response to God's
pilgrims have become comfortable with this approach. Now,
th mansion, they are being asked to let go of a good portion of
logical pursuits and rely on God alone. For those pilgrims who
to slowly release themselves from discovering God through
acad ia, the fourth mansion is the setting in which this radical change
will begin to take place. Cognitive analyzing merges into a loving
surrender to God's wisdom. A faith which was based on laws is now
becoming a faith based on love. Faith has reached a place where it can go
beyond understanding. There is less emphasis on rationalizing God into
what others have said or written about him or what one's own puny
cognitions have discovered about him. The pilgrims have run out of
questions simply because there are no answers that can adequately
describe the infinite God. They realize that there is a limit to understanding. There are no measurable ways in which to gauge the immensity
of God or his love. The mind of God is far beyond what any human can
fathom.

There is great difficulty in letting go of the known and seeking after
the unknown in ways that are strange and alien. Our pilgrims desire to
advance in faith and prayer through time-honored methods, but these
methods do not fit into the fourth mansion. It is scary to be in this mansion.
The pilgrims who cannot begin to let go are wrestling with minds that
keep whirring around continually giving them an endless list of reasons
not to let go. Sometimes these reasons seduce the pilgrims to abandon
prayer because this new prayer leaves nothing to grasp on to or nothing
in which to connect. There are no road maps, no specific procedures, and
no operational definitions. In their minds, our pilgrims may think that all
is now lost since there is no overt progression in prayer, and the time spent

with God seems so wasted. This rationalization occurs when one seeks to have an answer or explanation for everything. However, when our pilgrims have progressed over the bridge and realize that they are much closer to the center of the castle than they were before, they see the significance of not paying attention to their whirring minds. They also do not desire to investigate deeper into their former methods of prayer.

After some time has been spent in the fourth mansion, they find that they are not as concerned about disturbing and disrupting thoughts as they once were. The pilgrims have come to realize that these thoughts will diminish if undue attention is not lavished upon them. Teresa notes that interior battles, that is conflicts regarding any aspect of the human condition which takes place in the mind, are much more difficult to resolve and cause more stress and strain on the individual than external problems and difficulties. The mind can be a container for thoughts that are so negative, pessimistic and problematic that they could well lead to a psychological break from reality. Conversely, the mind can also be the seat of tranquility and peace that flows from God's love. The latter happens when a faith strong in the confidence of God and grounded in sincere simplicity is present in the heart. A faith that has a strong orientation in the intellect may be grounded in sophisticated complexity.

Let us pause for a while as we stand at the entrance to the fourth mansion and spend a short time reflecting on how a person's mind takes part in the development of prayer within the outer mansions. At this point a review may be refreshing, as it will give a greater clarity to the type of prayer that is to come.

Up to this point, all prayer that is experienced is discursive prayer. This means that there are activities within the mind that proceed from knowledge of one truth or an aspect of faith to knowledge of another truth or other aspect of faith. A passage from one spiritual point to another is made. There may be an analysis of all the events that happen, let us say, in a scene from scripture. Mental prayer in this context is stimulated by the who, what, when, where, and why of the particular biblical scene. We are pondering and visualizing the phrases and phases in the story line and thinking about the specific events. Then, there is an understanding which is enlightening. We take the enlightenment and integrate it so that practical conclusions can be drawn from it. The mind chooses what is useful and disregards the things that are not necessary points to remember in our own life style. We make resolutions which will alter the future so that we become more centered on the teachings of the biblical story. This prayer is good. There is absolutely nothing wrong with it, but we must be aware of the fact that the mind is very active here. Prayer is made, basically, through the imagination and cognitive processes. It requires work, effort, concentration and a firmness of resolve. It is all "doing" for God.

Two prayers which are very common in the first three mansions are prayers of petition and intercession. We petition God for our own needs and intercede for the needs of others. Both are a tremendous value. Nevertheless, they should not be abused, over used, seen as a magical cure for everything negative, or used as a simplistic answer to a difficult situation.

It is often said that "prayer is the answer," and rightly so. This is excellent advice, but oftentimes it does not directly meet the issue. Other adjunctive resources may need to be considered before an issue can be completely resolved. If a person is experiencing acute loneliness, combined with a deep, irrational fear for a long period of time, advising the person to pray and trust in God is only half of an answer and the easier half to be sure. Counseling from well-trained professionals is necessary in order to get at the root causes of the loneliness and fear. In therapy a skilled counselor works in union with the prayers offered, and a deeper healing takes place.

The college student who spends his time praying that he will pass his exam has taken the easy but not very practical road. He would do better to offer a short prayer, then use the brain that God gave him and really study the material that will be on the exam. The athletic team that prays to win had better make sure it is in tip top shape before the game begins. When a person is sick, it is good to pray, but it is also very advantageous to make an appointment with a competent physician. If a parish is looking forward to a very special eucharistic celebration and prays earnestly to God that everything will run smoothly, God is not to be blamed if the public address system does not work, or the lectors fumble their lines, or the recessional turns out to be a total disaster.

Prayers of petition and intercession are necessary and useful. There is no denying that! Although, on many occasions, they must go hand in hand with auxiliary assistance that faces the issue or problem directly. Prayer is not a mystical formula that automatically makes everything better. God uses those who have gifts and talents in specialized areas to assist us in our needs. Sometimes there is a fearful or dreadful anticipation when contacting an adjunctive person for the first time. In the struggles of life that initiate intercessory prayer, the prayer and the reaching out for help are prefixed with a reassurance that God gives us strength to do things that are beyond our own strength.

It is significant to note that authentic prayer, in whatever form it takes, can only flow from an emotional life that is stable. Emotional extremes are a great inhibitor to the spiritual life. Usually the normal events of life cause one's emotions to react to times of tranquility and times of trials in a cyclic way that does not fly off into extremes. These repetitive hills and valleys, if they fluctuate evenly, cause a healthy balancing within an individual and promotes an emotional growth toward wholeness. Being aware of one's own changing feelings establishes an ability to identify with the feelings of others in a more authentic way. This identity can nourish a faith that has corresponding hills and valleys. This type of faith is most at home in the heart. A faith that is most at home in the head may cause the person to spend hours and hours analyzing the causes behind the emotional fluctuations. Because of this, there then is a minimal or even no enjoyment of the pleasant rhythm of life that emotions bring. Those who scrutinize every aspect of a tree probably have great difficulty in enjoying the beauty of the forest.

It is important for our pilgrim to be aware of and in tune with his or her own ever changing emotions and feelings that mark the passing days. They can greatly affect the attitude a person has when going into prayer or even during prayer. No strong emotion or feeling, be it positive or negative, can be held for an indefinite length of time. When they are present, they can cause a great deal of internal havoc. A person is unable to beat emotions or feelings into a state of submission. They are as natural to life as eating and drinking. Thank God for them when they are experienced in an appropriate way. It would be hard to imagine an existence where everyone was in a chronic state of flat affect. How utterly dull and boring! Our pilgrim soon realizes that prayer is difficult when emotions or feelings are peaked at a positive or negative level. The charged emotional feeling is an inhibitor to prayer. One is usually caught up in the event that caused the peak instead of dwelling in the here and now of prayer. Negative emotional peaks can be evoked from a work day that is filled with unresolved problems, a very busy day, or a day that is psychologically upsetting in one way or another. There may be undue stress from physical or emotional pain, difficulty with a meaningful relationship, friction in the family or community, a disturbing event on the news, or just a continual commotion caused by noise, confusion, and the irksome ways of people. When one finds oneself overly occupied by these events at prayer, one should not try to force prayer at that time. If prayer is forced, it could well add to the stress and strain of the day. Instead of praying, it would be better to take a walk, take a nap, listen to soothing music, work on a crossword puzzle, read a spine-tingling, bloodchilling mystery novel, hammer a nail, sweep the patio, play with the dog, or do anything else that would help take the mind away from the disconcerting event of the day. By doing something out of the ordinary, an individual is placing distance between the cause of the emotional upset and the present moment. A person can resume praying sometime later on in the day when he or she is more at rest within. A homeostasis is found in active prayer when a watchful, recollected mind enters a quiet, feeling heart and mind and heart pray together.

Continual emotional extremes are dangerous and produce a blunting effect on an individual's emotional and spiritual development. It is also significant to note that preventing expression of one's emotions is likewise unhealthy. This type of inhibition springs from false courage and/or denial of feelings. There are two common approaches seen here: the macho man, and the woman who maintains a stiff upper lip. Both approaches are used because the person feels uncomfortable when his or her reaction to stress produces any personal feelings of inadequacy. A mistaken notion is that being unemotional means being strong and in control. Self-control is maintained at all costs. There is no excuse for temporarily leaning on another person. A person maintains a strong denial of needing others and a great fear of appearing weak to oneself. The behavioral term for this aberrancy is reaction formation. This is manifested in many forms. In our present context, we see how an overt display of emotion is personally and socially unacceptable to an individual. These emotions have been repressed to an unconscious level and replaced by a stoic self-control. An example is the clergy, religious or married persons who are having problems with their particular state in life, yet describe their vocation in glowing terms to friends. A sound emotional development is required for a sound life of prayer.

It is in the fourth mansion that there is an inter-mingling of natural and supernatural prayer. There are other terms which describe natural prayer. Some of them are already familiar. They are active prayer, discursive prayer and mental prayer. In essence they mean the same thing as natural prayer. Another word which describes this type of prayer is acquired prayer. All the labels given to this type of prayer indicate that in this prayer the person is actively communicating with God. To avoid undue confusion, from henceforth this type of prayer will be called active prayer.

Supernatural prayer is where God takes over. It is also called infused contemplation, passive prayer, mystical prayer, or infused prayer. All labels, again, essentially mean the same thing. This type of prayer means that God is communicating with the person. The person attains this prayer by not seeking it. There is a stillness and a quietness within, and a "being" for God in his presence. To avoid undue confusion, from henceforth this type of prayer will be referred to as passive prayer.

The criteria for assessing the difference between active and passive prayer depends on the attention, action and emphasis of the human partner. If a person is engaging in any form of active participation, even in the smallest possible way, when communing with God the prayer is active prayer. If the person is quietly aware of the presence of God, or if one feels as if one is being held by God, or absorbed by him, or suspended or immersed in him, the prayer is seemingly passive. Passive prayer is the prayer that is first experienced in the fourth mansion. It is being attentive to what God is doing. There is a cessation of an individual's energies and a direct contact with God himself through a peaceful relaxing in his embrace. The bridge that is symbolized in this mansion begins with self and ends in God. As our pilgrim travels across it, he or she experiences less and less of self and more and more of God. God comes to a person through this new type of prayer. He comes as himself, there is no created image of him. Passive prayer is a peaceful, internal response where the heart is captivated by the divine presence. In active prayer, the person gives to God. In passive prayer, God gives to the person. Passive prayer is, indeed, mystical for no speaking is involved here, only an attentive listening. It is a prayer of patience and waiting rather than a prayer of energy and power. The individuals in this mansion give up their own ideas about what holiness, faith and prayer are and allow God to be God in their lives. Prayer is a quiet resting in the mystery of God here. There is a very great awareness of God present in the internal true self radiating outward to the external boundaries of self.

Teresa said that in order to get to the fourth mansion, most of us must live for a very long time in the previous mansions. We must be willing to prepare ourselves in as generous a way as possible. There is to be a letting go of our ego-centered sense of worth, spirituality, importance and independence. We can contemplate ourselves in many ways. The lengthy stays in the first three mansions are a preparatory stage for this gradual releasing. If the preparation is worth its salt, the letting go is seen as a simple gift that is given to God without any thought of reciprocation. To be as a gift freely given to God with no strings attached is the only way we can survive after we have crossed the bridge. We cannot measure God by our own standards once we are on the other side of the bridge. From now on the new type of prayer that will come will require an endurance that has no returns. There is an awful lot of letting go in many areas within the fourth mansion!

Teresa gives us a lovely description to illustrate the difference between active and passive prayer. She was a great one to use simple things to get her point across. For this example she again uses her all-time favorite, water. There are two fountains. Both have a basin filled to the brim with cool, refreshing water. In one fountain the water comes to it through many miles of pipe. The source of the water for this fountain is a long distance away. There are several devices along the way which work to send the water toward the fountain. Much effort is involved in getting the water to the fountain. This fountain is like active prayer. Something from the outside is initiating prayer. Inspiration comes through the senses and brings the desire to pray from the outside to the inside. The sources of this prayer are myriad. They could come through a spiritual book, a flower in bloom, a beautiful picture, church bells, chanting, or the natural scent of a pine forest or a prairie. They could be written prayers of praise and thanksgiving offered to God in heaven. God in heaven also implies distance. Like the water source, active prayer implies a distance and a "giving to." The effort in active prayer is in responding to the flow of graces that comes from different sources and in offering prayers to God. It parallels the water working its way to the fountain.

The second fountain has its water source very close. The water flowing into the fountain comes from a spring right under the fountain. The water from the source is one with water in the fountain. No energy, labor or technology is used to bring the source of the water to the fountain. The two waters blend as one. There is no difference between the water from the source and the water in the basin. This fountain resembles passive prayer. It is an awareness of God being within that a person cannot really explain.

To be informed and aware

Because active prayer will continue to remain a viable part of one's prayer life, Teresa explains for us in detail the gifts that God gives to those in both active and passive prayer in the fourth mansion. She presents the similarities and differences of these gifts. The gifts associated with active prayer are called spiritual consolations. Spiritual delights can only be found in passive prayer.

Consolation comes from the Spanish word *contentos,* which translated means: contented, satisfied, joyful, peaceful, and other related pleasant experiences. These are the experiences felt by the person during or after prayer or any other element related to the spiritual life. Spiritual consolations are natural, acquired sensations that evolve from prayer, meditation, leading a God-centered life, or engaging in good works that assist others. They are very similar to corresponding feelings that result from the pleasant events of daily life. A pleasant satisfaction is felt after a job is well done. A peacefulness is experienced after a difficult problem has been resolved. Feelings and consolations require some activity in order to be initiated. They are also felt more intensely when unexpected events permeate a well-planned, ordinary day. Much happiness comes from finding out that a person has inherited a large sum of money from a far distant relative, and much happiness comes when a person attended a retreat with no expectations and found many graces and blessings. There is an overwhelming joy when one has seen a dear friend unexpectedly, and there is an overwhelming joy when an event in the life of Christ has been pondered for a long time then understood in a new way. A family feels a great sense of relief when a member who is in the military and listed as missing in action for several months has been found safe and sound. A great sense of relief is felt when an individual has been reconciled with God after he or she has just finished a rather difficult confession. The regular consolations in the events of everyday life and the spiritual consolations in one's life with God are almost parallel. Both are given to us through God's creative gifts to us. They are a part of human nature which balances out the discouraging and disheartening events in life.

Delights come from the Teresian Spanish word *gustos.* This word encompasses all feelings that are pleasurable. Spiritual delights resemble spiritual consolations because they are very similar in the felt sense, but there is a distinct difference in the origin and source of the spiritual delights. Delights are infused mystical gifts from God that come directly from God. No human event nor any element in human nature can initiate them. Spiritual delights can only be present when God is acting on the individual in a special way. Delights do not come through any methods or any preconceived imaginings of God. Spiritual delights are first experienced in the fourth mansion. There is no way in which they could be sustained within any of the outer mansions. They begin in God and are given to individuals as he pleases.

It is through passive prayer and spiritual delights that what Teresa identifies as the "expansion of the heart" happens. During "expansions" a person's heart feels flooded with God. The flood flows through one and permeates every fiber of one's being. It then overflows into an individual's outlook on life. At this early stage this event happens unconsciously. The person is not aware of what is happening until after the experience is over. It is a fleeting, momentary event and the person cannot even wonder what is going on. One just lovingly accepts. There are no explanations. What has happened can only be illustrated by examples. These "expansions" which follow delights, when experienced for the first time, could not even be imagined before they took place. Through them God is drawing an individual closer to himself in a way that is known only to him.

In a way, spiritual consolations, if they are not appropriately connected with God, have a slightly different effect on the heart. They may cause it to constrict instead of dilate. This only occurs in some cases, but it is worthwhile to mention it here as a precautionary measure. Let us say that a person becomes so awestruck by a potent passage in scripture that he or she is moved to tears of joy. These tears come through a sudden understanding of this passage. The passage has been grappled with for weeks and understanding it is a great relief. The tears flow and flow. At last, enlightenment! Soon a headache is felt. The headache turns out to be a painful migraine. What effect does this have on the heart? It turns the heart inward to focus on an individual's discomfort. Now pain comes into the picture. In one's humanness, the pain is very present. It shadows the joy felt and places that joy in the background. Here we observe how the heart can become constricted with this type of consolation.

There are other ways in which spiritual consolations can take one off the path of prayer. A person is used to experiencing joy and pleasantness at prayer, and prayer is looked forward to as a time when he or she is able to float in a heavenly daze or linger in a euphoric state. Is this raw prayer, or the individual's own conceptualizations of prayer? It seems as if this person is accustomed to experiencing the pleasantries of prayer rather than working at or resting in the prayer itself. This type of consolation apparently builds from a person's fantasy of what prayer should be like as opposed to what prayer actually is in its stark reality. Many emotional responses are stimulated by one's own human nature and temperament. An individual needs an injection of humility to understand that pleasant emotional responses in prayer do not take him or her higher on the ladder of prayer, nor do they make a person more pleasing to God. These emotional responses are much like the devout feelings first felt in the second mansion. They stem from the intellect and from other activities of the mind. One rejoices in the good feelings that come through loving God. These are good, but they are not components of the fourth mansion. Unauthentic consolations come from the person and are directed back to the person. Spiritual consolations are good if they are not carried over into extended emotional amenities. They are a very real part of the spiritual life. They are experienced early in the spiritual life and will continue to be experienced up to and including the seventh mansion. However inspiring they may be, they are not to be confused with spiritual delights. Spiritual delights blossom in the fourth mansion where loving in prayer overrides feelings associated with prayer. This love does not consist in many consolations or delights, or many words or holy thoughts. It is a selfless love that loves the other for the sake of the other. Teresa says that this is loving the God of consolations rather than the consolations of God. It is loving God without thoughts, words, feelings or gratifications. Faith grows when a person does not rely on receiving spiritual consolations but finds joy in giving consolations to others in a Mary-like manner.

It is important to remember that our pilgrim in the fourth mansion is only at the beginning stages of passive prayer. Thinking much is slowly changing into loving much. The pilgrim gradually lets the intellect go and surrenders all into the arms of love. Distractions and the wandering mind are very much a part of this transitory stage. They are a part of the human condition and cannot be avoided. Not much concern is given to their removal in this mansion. There is also a fluctuation between active and passive prayer. Active prayer will not fade away. It will be used continually throughout the spiritual journey.

The prayer of recollection seems to be a beneficial connecting bond between active prayer and preparation for passive prayer. Recollection prepares us to listen and attentive listening enables God to work in us. This prayer is known by its simplicity. It is based on love. Teresa emphasizes that we should do whatever we can in order to bring us to a loving presence before God. She cautions that this in no way should be an arduous task, nor is it to cause a restlessness due to our own efforts. Recollection does not consist of many words. If we are continually repeating "God, I love you, I love you, I love you" in our minds, how can we listen to him? Here, all loving is gentle and peaceful. Sometimes loving can come simply by leaving everything to God in prayer. Teresa says that at this point any toilsome expression of love would cause more harm than good. Conversely, if we are busy trying not to think of ways of loving, that act in itself could well arouse the mind to think more. Recollection is best when it is without endeavors, effort, or explanations. There is no need to work, so no effort is required. This prayer is not intense. It quietly desires to rest in God alone. It is a help to be empty, open, receptive and accepting to what God wants within. It is being sensitive to a greater interior spiritual dimension and risking vulnerability to whatever God has in store. In recollection we pray best when we do not realize we are praying at all.

A prelude to passive prayer can also be made through the many gateways that lead us to a state of relaxation. A few examples are: soft music, mantras, centering, controlled breathing, guided imagery, specific relaxation techniques, tai ch'i, sufi dancing, zen or yoga. All these, if done in a Christian perspective, lead to a seeking of the Christ within.

Events that seem to be looked upon as adverse incidents in our lives can be forerunners of the first kind of passive prayer. Some of these conditions may include: periods of dryness in prayer, some type of crisis in our life journey, a lack of meaning in our work, a stagnation in a loving relationship, a series of painful frustrations, a feeling of being out of sorts for no apparent reason, a sense of weakness or failure, a terrible event we do not care to think about, a time of transition, or a severe illness. As catastrophic as these examples may seem, they may prove to be a gateway that opens us up to the first stage of passive prayer. This initial prayer is called the prayer of quiet.

The prayer of quiet is our pilgrim's first encounter with a prayer that is beyond words, concepts, or other prayer-oriented paraphernalia that pass through the mind. This prayer is important in one's journey because it represents a significant change in the way in which one prays. It is not accomplished by an individual's own ironclad determination, nor is there a conscious awareness of God. Rather it is being filled with God's presence from the inside out and letting this presence flow on and further outward into one's relationships with others.

The prayer of quiet generally can be described as a prayer of deep stillness, profound peace, interior calm and a very serene recollection. These, combined with a placid joy, well up from the very depths of one's inmost heart where God alone resides. It is not an atmosphere within, but a very real felt sensing of something tangible within that is very difficult to describe. Its source is God. It comes from God, and it takes on various expressions in different people.

After this type of prayer, oftentimes a pilgrim cannot understand what has happened or what he or she has received. The prayer of quiet is not specific as to time. No signs say when it has begun or when it has ended. It may be as insignificant as a passing sigh or as profound as a gentle invasion by God. There is nothing a person can do to duplicate the prayer or repeat the felt experience so it can happen again. An individual cannot will or desire it into being. In this prayer there is a definite loss of time. That is why it is difficult to tell how long the prayer lasts. There are many levels of experience in the prayer of quiet. A pilgrim has no control of the time spent within this prayer or the level of soft intensity he or she experiences at this prayer. The prayer of quiet is neither a permanent state nor is it always filled with spiritual delights. However, this is the prayer in which spiritual delights are first recognized for what they are. Usually one comes out of this prayer when one realizes that one is praying. This prayer happens when an individual least expects it. All the interior faculties, the mind, the will, the intellect, the memory, the imagination and the senses that were like rushing rivers within a person's head are now quieted down and become as placid pools of deep tranquility. A pilgrim is caught up and absorbed in a joy that is delicate and fragile, a silence that is pregnant and profound, and a peace that flows from the rich, unknown center of his or her existence. Because of the subtleness of this prayer, there is no understanding of the favors God has given one. There is only an intensification of belief in his unfathomable love, a deepening of humility and a desire not to talk about the experiences one has had. An individual knows well that such gifts are not rewards for good behavior or a sign that he or she has been singularly blessed by God.

A precaution should be mentioned at this point. During the prayer of quiet, we may notice that we are hardly breathing or not breathing at all. Since we are in a quieted state, there is no big crisis nor cause for the red alarm. We do not desire to lose this state of tranquility, so we automatically resume breathing with no gasping or great exhalations. It is as simple as that. Breathing is resumed as gently as it was stopped.

Well now, all this in the fourth mansion is very new, wondrous and delightful, and our pilgrims' curiosity is peaked. If everything in the prayer of quiet is so mysterious, nebulous and elusive, how can they tell if they have genuinely prayed in this quiet prayer?

Several signposts point to an authentic practice of the prayer of quiet or any other prayer within the passive prayer category. When we are actually praying in the prayer of quiet, the familiar ways of prayer and meditation are difficult if not impossible. This is due to the mystical nature of this prayer. Within the prayer of quiet we experience God as a whole, total being. There are no conceptualizations of any specific elements that make up his being. We do not break God up into different categories such as: God is Love, God the Creator, God of Beauty, God of Wisdom, God all Powerful, Merciful God, Father God, or the many other elements of God. There is just God is God, *Deus est.*

We may feel that our love for God has diminished. There is not the joy and delight previously felt in meditation and other forms of active prayer. We feel dry, and when we think of God or his created things we experience desolation, distaste and discomfort.

There is a strong desire to be alone and a perpetual need for prayer despite the previously mentioned feelings. We do not shirk daily family, work or social duties. They are done well and in a cheerful manner. After they are finished, we sense a gravitation toward quiet, leisure time activities through which we sincerely seek God despite a lack of fervor. A loving attention to God flows from an unknown source in the heart rather than from sources that are associated with the negative feelings we may be experiencing at the moment. When an unexpected task or event of our state of life requires our presence during our quiet activities, this same loving attention calls us to respond to it with care and goodwill.

After our pilgrims have felt their first touch of God's delights, all events within their lives shift around and take on a new perspective. During the times of passive prayer, there are no thoughts of problems, pains, worries, trials, troubles or anything else that sets their teeth on edge. When they emerge from prayer, everything is put into its proper perspective in relation to God and the things of God. God is most important, and all restless desires, urgent longings, and unanswered questions take on an insignificance that was unknown before. Through these loving delights from God, all troublesome events that occur during daily life are not as bothersome nor do they take up as much space in the mind as they previously did.

Because everything is so new and awesome, Teresa gives a strong warning to those traveling in the fourth mansion. She exhorts her travelers not to place themselves in situations where they can turn away from God's love. This is their first experience of mystical prayer. Teresa likens these pilgrims to nursing babes here. If these infants turn away from the source of their nourishment, what can they expect but death? If our pilgrims turn away from prayer at this point, it would be as if their spiritual throats were cut. Since they are at the beginning of a new phase in prayer, it is very easy to slip into a pseudo praying state. Prayer is false when these new delights become an end in themselves rather than a means to an end. Prayer is false when an individual becomes prideful and pompous because he or she has experienced these spiritual delights. Prayer is false when one thinks one is uniquely favored by God. Vocal prayer is false when there is a self-centered concern about how one looks or sounds to others. If an individual has leanings toward pseudo prayer, it would be well to remember the virtue that runs through each mansion like a golden thread. This thread steadily grows stronger, and at the end it is firmly anchored in the heart of Christ who resides at the center of the interior castle. This virtue is humility which is based on the stark realization, acceptance and dependence on God's mercy. Humility grows through the slow stripping away of the many layers of self.

This is still a painful process! Our pilgrims remember that humility is a continuous process that goes on in each mansion. Many layers of self can accumulate if there is an adverse expression of self-sufficiency. This adverseness is the notion that one is able to meet one's own needs with only a minimal need of God. This point is being brought forth now because our pilgrims may inherit this adversity through their new found prayer. They may think they are super strong because they have been especially favored. Such notions are a mistake. We can see living examples of an adverse expression of self-sufficiency when we glance back at the palace of perfect persons in the third mansion.

Actually, it is from these people that the palace gets it name. Among the other residents of the third mansion these residents are known as Mr. or Ms. Perfect. They look as if they stepped out of a Bullock's Wilshire or a Sak's Fifth Avenue fashion catalogue. They seem happy. They may have a smug or snobbish manner, but they are usually not even aware of it. They have always known wealth, associate with high society, and have the best there is within all realms of existence. They may be demanding and critical. This seems to develop from being so in control and self-assured of everything. These people take pride in their radical independence and are pleased because they do not require any assistance from others save the butler and the maid. Mr. or Ms. Perfect are set apart from the rest of the permanent residents in the third mansion because they have a repugnance toward any good work that is directed toward anyone who does not fit in their social setting. They shy away from working among the sick, poor, abused, mentally impaired, unwanted, homeless, malnourished or any other group of people that experience oppression. They dread visiting loved ones in a hospital because they find the environment distasteful. These people are content with helping in activities that fit easily and securely into the life styles in which they are familiar. It seems apparent that they have not learned to trust others because the need for dependency on others has never been present within their lives. A strong self-sufficiency also prevents trusting relationships to exist. If their trust in others, whom they can see, is found wanting, how can they build trust in God whom they cannot see?

Growth through the third mansion cannot take place until a person is able to trust. Often total abandonment to God is learned through an unexpected, traumatic event that alters one's life style. Mr. or Ms. Perfect have not experienced any moderate or severe setbacks within any area of their lives. Because of their fierce independence, their relationship with God is not one hallmarked by a loving dependence. This results in an adverse self-sufficiency which is like a centripetal force that holds one together. God is a part of their lives, yes, but these people relate to him in a formal, business-like manner. Authentic humanness comes through a person who is dependent on God and interdependent on others. Interdependence represents a gentle centrifugal force that connects people together in their need for each other.

Another danger Teresa cautions against in the fourth mansion is the tendency to get caught up in the spiritual delights. Here a person floats in them and extends these delights time-wise and depth-wise far beyond what God actually had in mind. Teresa saw this tendency as a weakness comparable to a state of lethargy. A languid, listless attitude is no good for one's health. In fact, it wears it down through atrophy. These individuals think they are experiencing something greater than what God is actually giving them and get very absorbed in their own exaggerated fantasies. Teresa calls this absolute nonsense since it amounts to nothing more than wasting time and living in a contrived state of reality. What would one do with a person who remained in a state of "rapture" for eight hours? Call the men in the white coats most likely, for in this bogus state the person experiences no sensory input, nor does he or she experience anything that concerns God. The person resembles an individual who is closer to sustaining a psychotic state rather than an authentic mystical awareness. If something is truly a spiritual delight from God, the person receiving it will not experience any internal or external languishings. Nor will the peak experience be for a long duration. God's delights usually last for a very short time in the fourth mansion. If one is aware that one's mind is being taken up with flights of fancy that embellish or extend God's gifts, it would be advantageous to get busy with the ordinary duties of the day as soon as the flights become apparent. A person should also take care that he or she does not work alone for this could exacerbate the problem. Such flights of fancy may be an indication that one is using "holy happenings" as an excuse for subconscious procrastination, nourishing a melancholic state, or finding an excuse so that one does not have to work. It can also be a sign of deep-seated emotional problems.

The fourth mansion is where our pilgrims receive their first taste of spiritual poverty. The nature of prayer in this mansion demands a stark surrender to God. There is a laying aside of familiar, comfortable prayerful practices. There is a release of the need to feel in control of one's spiritual life and all the activities within it. The unknown regions of the fourth mansion are explored with a blinding trust in God. It is here that our pilgrims learn how to become passive and receptive to God. There is a feeling of helplessness and great vulnerability before God. It does not bother our pilgrims that they do not comprehend what is happening. They find out new things about themselves that they never were aware of and are amazed at these discoveries. The criteria of their prayer lives is based on their lives outside of prayer. The primary way they learn to pray is by praying and trying to be wide open to God during their prayers. The pilgrims' passive and receptive disposition to God opens them up to a passive and receptive disposition to others. The disposition finds expression in an emerging tenderness. Hurry is a diminishing element in their lives while a tenderness, deftness, and sureness gives them a greater capacity to pay less attention to trivial things and more attention to listening to and being with others. Our pilgrims now realize the love of God is dependent on love of themselves and love of others. Seeing Christ in the eucharist can only result from seeing Christ in themselves and seeing him in others.

What are some of the landmarks that show our sensitivity to Christ in others? It becomes easier to put up with the quirks and foibles of those around us. An honest respect is shown toward anyone with whom we come in contact. Laughter comes with ease about ourselves and with others. Consideration and courtesy underline our social interactions. There is a conscientious effort not to take anyone for granted. We endeavor to resolve any anger before the sun sets. Meals become times for sharing—something old, something new, or the best and worst events of the day—rather than a time for watching TV or listening to the stereo. When a scolding is necessary, the admonitions are directed toward the action, rather than the person behind the action. We learn to erase quickly with an apology ugly, hasty, angry, black words that could leave a lasting hurt on others. When our dark side seems to dominate the day, we may wear a crab pin to warn others of impending trouble. We may wish to make a list of ways to show tenderness toward those with whom we live, then give overt expression to the items on the list. There are interior challenges that can be set up that aim at seeing Christ in others. We may resolve to utter no words of complaint for three hours. If this is successful, the hours increase to five, then maybe a whole day. No frowns, groans, and sighs of displeasure are shown when we are performing tasks that go against the grain. We may say something pleasant to each person we speak with during the day and eliminate one inconsistency during the week. We attend a meeting even though there are five good reasons why it would be better to stay at home and relax. For all the western folk and others who gather around the campfire to the tune of "Home on the Range" all may create an environment where "seldom is heard a discouraging word." Because we are learning how to transcend ourselves, we find that when visiting a nursing home the smell of urine that used to make us gag is not as nauseating as it once was. Even though we are not fond of writing letters, a letter goes off to a far distant friend or to one who is housebound. New clothes may be desired, but the old ones are not worn out so the money is sent, perhaps anonymously, to a worthy cause. We may say prayers for people who have a tendency to rub us the wrong way. We are learning to give and receive graciously, gratefully and lovingly. Through becoming more open to God's workings within, we become more generous. There is a disregard of our own wants and desires so we can be available to others. There is a challenge to look beyond our own family or community and stretch our love to include the entire human family. The beauty and grandeur of God is revealed to us in all his creation. Life is approached with a sense of wonder, reverence and integrity. We look about and find everything Christ-ed with love, giving glory to God.

I see his blood upon the rose
And in the stars the glory of his eyes
His body gleams amid eternal snows,
His tears fall from the skies.

I see his face in every flower.
The thunder and the singing of the birds
Are but his voice—and carven by his power
Rocks are his written words.

All pathways by his feet are worn,
His strong heart stirs the ever-beating sea,
His crown of thorns is twined with every thorn.
His crown in every tree.

Joseph M. Plunkett

Inside the fourth mansion our pilgrims sense an interior freedom that comes along with the transformation in prayer. There is no longer an intense hold on programmed prayer practices. Fear of the unknown is accepted and faced with a sturdy belief in God's goodness. The person who was once cautious and fearful of doing anything new has really learned to trust in God. All the anxieties that haunted the people in the third mansion have diminished. Our pilgrims march into the unknown despite their fears. They have learned that fear is a part of courage. Rational fears become less frightening because they are now faced with faith. Faith is more alive. The pilgrims have become more confident in God and desire to do all things in God. This liberation is like a fresh balmy breeze on a hot, still day.

Our pilgrims also experience a sense of fragility. Since these new found spiritual delights are so new, the pilgrims feel, to a greater extent, their clumsiness and incoordination when walking along the spiritual path. They fear these awkward elements may disrupt or detract from the tenderness in which the spiritual delights should be received. There is no need to worry here. If God thought that it was a mistake to extend his favors to pilgrims who saw themselves as clumsy, he would not have done so in the first place. They do not need to be still and silent in order to reduce the chances of bungling things up. In time, this fear will be resolved and feelings of deep gratitude, love and amazement will take its place.

As our pilgrims travel in the fourth mansion they will find that Teresa does not give any specific step by step techniques or methods within any particular type of prayer. There is no intellectual approach to insure them that a particular type of prayer has been mastered. She does not offer point systems to indicate that growth in a certain prayer has taken place. There are no methods for meditation that would produce a desired effect in mental prayer. Prayer requires a giving up of interest and attention that is given to oneself. In order to open themselves to God the pilgrims must let go of all the measuring devices they have picked up along the spiritual path. They cannot capture God by contrived capers. If they seek to capture God, he may become more elusive than ever for this is not prayer. Instructions regarding how to pray, explicit desires within specific states of prayer, emotional needs that prayer satisfies, and other related matters are not a part of prayer in this mansion. God is truly loved when there are no motives used that are associated with spiritual self-gratification. Prayer is simply lived.

The relaxed grasp

In the fourth mansion the pilgrims begin to encounter the passion of Jesus. Passive prayer is desired with sincere ardor. It is not wrong to desire this. However, it cannot be acquired by persons seeking it. The pilgrims' only desire should be to let God be God and realize his desire to give himself to them in his own time. If delights do not come, there is no need to fret for the only real desire that is necessary is union of one's own will with the will of God. Delights or no delights, it does not matter. To walk on the path of love is to desire to serve the crucified Christ, and let him do whatever he likes. People in the fourth mansion forfeit their desire to know if they really have received spiritual delights. They sacrifice the security they think these delights will give them. Sacrifice is also seen in the longing to know where our pilgrims are, or how they have grown, on the spiritual journey. There is sacrifice in the desire to experience the spiritual delights again. From all this evolves a deep trust in God. Trust is strongly held on to, especially when nothing seems to be happening and prayer seems to be empty.

Yes, prayer is encountered in a new form, but it can also become a bleak experience. We begin our time set apart for personal solitary prayer with good desires and intentions. Almost immediately there is nothing that follows. We may read a spiritual book for enlightenment for a short time. It is put aside and again there is nothing. We feel like a bump on a log. Everything is inert. There is a coldness and distance from everything spiritual. The time passes very slowly. The sounds of traffic, planes, the ticking of the clock all seem louder than usual. We are very aware of our posture and begin to fidget or squirm, crazy thoughts assault the mind. Where is God? There is nothing. How can we find a new path of communication to him? There is still nothing. No sign around or within speaks of his presence. There is only blackness. There seems to be no value connected with this time set aside for prayer. There are many things to do and everything is bombarding the mind with "Do it now!"

It is when our pilgrims are faced with this situation that many of them give up on prayer. The reason is not that they do not want to pray. It is because they desire that their prayer be more interesting, more relevant, more meaningful, more exciting, more dynamic, more vivacious. Then there would be "something" to go on. Yet this "something" is not as worthwhile as these people think. It was only a step back into a former way of prayer when they understood what was happening and had control. To step forward is to be content with the darkness of prayer in the fourth mansion. This is painful since it is insecure, meaningless, boring and not at all satisfying. So be it. Our pilgrims have choices to make. They can sink to their previous safe and sane levels of prayer that are known or swim ahead into the dark, mysterious waters of prayer that are unknown. True faith shines forth when our pilgrims come to their times of prayer day after day, month after month, year after year with no thoughts of the joys or fears that may be associated with prayer. This is letting God pass out of one's own speculations and be himself. It is being loyal to one's tryst with him even when he does not seem to be there.

It is important to note here that the tender spiritual delights of God will not be felt every time our pilgrims pray. There must be a guard against expecting them for they may be a once in a lifetime experience or as rare as a clear day in a city frequently strangled by smog. Our pilgrims should also guard against comparing and/or contrasting passive prayer times with everyday, ordinary, run-of-the-mill active prayer times. Judgments, assumptions or inferences concerning which prayer is the best prayer are absolutely out. No level of prayer is continuous. Yes, there are times when our pilgrims feel overwhelmed with God's love and desire to share this love with others. Such are the peak experiences in prayer. Our pilgrims feel enlightened, enthusiastic, fervent and filled to the brim with everything that is good. Yet, there are other times when prayer is as dry as a bone and there is the temptation to despair. God has left. The pilgrims feel totally empty. They feel as if they are at the bottom of the pit of life, so what is the use of going on? They cry out to God, "I hate your guts, and I would be better off without you." There are two sides to the picture, and our pilgrims would not desire it any differently. There is to be an acceptance and an embracing of both. Teresa said that, in essence, prayer does not consist of good or bad feelings but of strong determination, and it is alright to be mad at him during troublesome time. Picture one of our pilgrims sitting on the bank of a river. The waters flow evenly by. The water represents favorable times in prayer and not so favorable times in prayer. (It can also represent all the events that flow through life.) Watch the river. Embrace each prayer time and each event as it comes along, then let go of it. "All things are passing." An old Zen proverb goes something like this:

> One chops firewood.
> One carries water.
> One reaches a stage of enlightenment.
> One continues to chop wood for the fire.
> One continues to carry water.

It is very easy to replace "enlightenment" with "confusion" in this proverb, or we could also replace it with "delights" or "dryness." Things would remain the same. There are good times and there are bad times. Such is the fiber of life. The only disaster that would disrupt the flow of life would be to stop praying.

As our pilgrims learn to love God without self-interest, a real sense of intimacy develops within friendships. Feelings and opinions are respected. Failings are easily forgiven. Areas of goodness are admired and sincerely emulated. There is a heartfelt caring for the other. One is more concerned about the friend's happiness than one's own. The concern is continual expressing itself week after week and year after year. Heartfelt care initiates the freedom to be vulnerable, and open, and trusting. The friend can be his or her own self in the deepest sense. There is no pretense or putting on airs. The friends feel profoundly at home with each other. Continual conversations become less necessary, and there is a contentment of just being in the calm company of the other. A gentle harmony exists between verbal dialogue and shared quiet. Often the loving acceptance and understanding felt in silent communication speaks louder than words. As in prayer, the silence allows for an intimate listening and a speech that is from heart to heart. In this mansion a person loves God and friend with a deep level of each one's own individuality. Friend is as friend, as God is as God.

Yes, the fourth mansion is the first encounter with God as he is. It is for those people who are mature, responsible, sincere and genuine in their efforts to lead wholesome, well-integrated lives. All the virtues mentioned in the earlier mansions are taken more seriously and become more intrinsic to the pilgrims. The fourth mansion is similar to the second mansion. Both signify new beginnings and new experiences. There is much letting go of the comforts our pilgrims have felt. In the second mansion these were in the material world. In the fourth mansion it is in the world of prayer. Now passive prayer will augment active prayer. Also, the pilgrims find that because they are more sensitive to God, they are more aware of themselves. A deeper realization that they are capable of committing every kind of evil is present. There is a greater sensitivity to destructive tendencies and behaviors that can harm authenticity in their relationship to themselves and to others. They see plenty of previously unrecognized deficits with which to confront. The single-mindedness that propels our pilgrims through the fourth mansion will uncover many negatives that point toward self-interest. There is a greater vulnerability and openness to the promptings of the Holy Spirit which make the pilgrims more alive to decisions made that are directed toward themselves or others. They become more aware of how selfless every word and action was within Jesus' life. They cannot help but notice their great number of flaws when comparing his life to their own. Jesus is our pilgrims' stronghold as they focus on the lifelong effort of love.

Midway in the fourth mansion prayer evolves from a daily task. Saying our prayers, or getting our prayers in, or seeing prayer as a duty to perform no longer are adequate reasons for praying. Prayer becomes a loving service that is essential to our being. In the recesses of our hearts prayer is an honor and privilege. We pray because we want to, not because we have to. Since difficulty in prayer is now a very real part of prayer, discipline is tightly interwoven with determination. This exercise in self-control supports and sustains us when we are present for prayer, but God is seemingly absent. Discipline is like a strong frame on which the continuous learning within prayer is built. It involves forgoing other interests, preparation, time, persistence, and constant conversion. Often we find that some aspect of family life, community, work, ministry, or some other necessity seems more important than prayer. When completing these tasks the time for prayer slips by. In retrospect, at the end of the day we find that those tasks could have been postponed without any harm. Discipline expressed in gentle firmness will help keep the events of daily life in correct order. Discipline will be the force behind the completion of the tasks that fill the days. Discipline will keep all things in moderation.

The fourth mansion opens us up to what God has to say. Prayer expands into an intense listening, and this is not possible without strong personal discipline. Faith calls us from sentiment, emotions, intellect or structures related to God to trust, honesty, silence and presence in God. The fourth mansion is a beginning. We begin to look beyond our own limited perspective of life into the total reality of life. We release the growth inhibitors in our past and take hold of our own unique journey. We move beyond seeing the externals of others in order to touch their interior goodness. We travel beyond our own space and time and actual existence into the eternity and immensity of God. Through our journey within the fourth mansion we find that God has become very personal, and we feel completely at home with him. We begin to appreciate deeply the wisdom of the listening Mary, woman of faith, as she lived with her beloved husband and Son, in precious intimacy, at Nazareth.

Fifth Mansion

FRAGMENTS OF HEAVEN

Teresa decides not to tell her pilgrims what awaits them within the rooms of the fifth mansion. She does not attempt to explain the treasures in these rooms because they are past understanding through reasoning or comprehending through illustrations. This mansion cannot be understood by any means of human endeavor. Neither the mind nor any other human faculty can shed light on what happens here. Any type of human cognition fails dramatically for the spiritual delights and the prayer in this mansion are too refined to be matched with any temporal beauty even in its highest form.

The fifth mansion is a mansion of many levels. Each level represents a different degree and a different interpretation of one of the manifold supernatural gifts of God. There is no need to experience every level within this mansion to insure that one has successfully passed through it. For some, it is enough to stand in the vestibule. For others, they are content by being aware of a few spiritual delights in a midsection of this mansion. God shows his mercy and showers his delights to different pilgrims in different ways. In this mansion, as in the previous mansions, the only way the pilgrims can become truly receptive to any of these delights is to strive to live, work, pray, play and love as Jesus did. At this point this is no idle thought or occasional musing. An honest day by day and hour by hour effort is directed toward becoming like Jesus in thought, word and deed. This is happening below the conscious level. It is a second nature. The pilgrims find that they are often saying to themselves during the course of the day, "Is this the way Jesus would have reacted?" They find that there are many times when the answer is no, but our pilgrims do not become discouraged. They simply pick themselves up and start over again. The resolution to do better is sincere and from the heart. There are no careless, casual, overt explanations about how they have failed. There is just a quiet realization that they have stepped outside of love and an offering of a tacit plea to God for help to do better in the future.

Teresa tells us that physical strength and stamina are not necessary for advancement in the spiritual life. All God asks is that we work the best we can with what we have. The pastor going about zealously in his round of parish activities, and the old woman sitting in a nursing home, confused and disoriented, can both love deeply with their hearts and give what they have to give. God is content with them both as he is content with all people who love him and fit within the different levels of daily activities. Taking the time to love God is more important to him than using our time to do a multitude of work for him. To love God greatly during one's confusion is of more worth to him than loving him in a small way during one's hectic schedule.

The fifth mansion is the mansion where the prayer of union takes place. It is often called the mansion of the prayer of union. Teresa notes that this prayer is experienced by only a few, and these few must continually work with themselves in order that God may work directly with them. As far as external deportment is concerned, these people are shining examples of what it means to be Christians, but these people are not fooled. Internally they know they have defects and flaws that eat away at their virtues and merits. These parasitical gnawings are evident because the individuals are sincerely working to make themselves more presentable in the loving eyes of God. This is done because the prayer of union represents a serious engagement before marriage. In terms of human understanding, the fifth mansion and the prayer in it may be viewed as a time of betrothal, as it was known in New Testament times.

Teresa describes the fifth mansion as a place where our pilgrim can enjoy fragments of heaven while he or she is still living on earth. When a person experiences the delights in this mansion, it is as if the individual is neither awake nor asleep. There is no realization of external things or events or awareness of the physical self. During the prayer of union, it seems as if one has left one's senses, thoughts, interior faculties and all other elements of one's personhood. There is no utilization of a person's imagination, intellect, will or sensory perceptions. The person is so caught in God's love that it seems he or she has left the body and has become one with God's love. During this suspension one is unaware of one's energies. There is no fatigue and no personal effort involved. The prayer of union is an intimate union of the person with God which is accompanied by a certainty of his presence within his or her own spirit. With this prayer there is an absence of distractions, since the person is entirely absorbed in God. In the prayer of union, the individual is being transformed in God. This lasts longer and is more profound than in the prayer of quiet. The prayer of union is only experienced at its beginning stages in the fifth mansion. The person becomes more receptive to God here and in a more comprehensive way. The spiritual delights in this mansion cause our pilgrims to be left with an ardent zeal to glorify God. An extraordinary experience of joy is also felt, combined with a desire for perfect submission to God's will. The spirit of the person relaxes and becomes softer and more consenting, conforming itself to his will. The depth of one's spirit is in a great peace.

God does not make himself present to the pilgrim in a way that can be logically explained in the prayer of union. He comes into the core of the person as Jesus came into the upper room and gave peace to his apostles after he rose from the dead. God has been within a person, and that individual can neither forget this experience nor, from a faith stance, doubt it.

There is no possible way in which the effects of this prayer can be imagined or explained. When a person comes out of this state and his or her human stance takes over, there can be doubts and suspicions regarding the authenticity about what has happened. Nothing is wrong with these self-doubts or questions. Even in this mansion, Teresa tells us that there are still self-deceptions and illusions. Self-examination makes our pilgrim human. Dubious thoughts about the actuality of the prayer of union do no harm if not much thought is paid to them. If a person was one hundred percent sure that the experience was real and from God, that person may become boastful and arrogant. If a person occasionally thinks that such an experience was imagined, dreamed or the result of wishful thinking, that person remains delightfully human. Indeed, one still retains one's humanity after such an experience has taken place. Because this experience is unexplainable, it would be wise to venture the sharing of such an event cautiously. The true purpose and reasoning behind the prayer of union are held in secret by God alone.

There is one way in which a pilgrim knows that this union with God is valid. During the prayer of union God places himself very deeply inside the innermost center of a person. When the person returns to a normal state, there is no way in which he or she could doubt that it was actually God within this interior. The certitude that God was there comes from God but, again, there is no way to prove that it was God within. One believes this strongly from a faith perspective, although at times one occasionally wavers from a human perspective. To become more holy is to become more human.

In this mansion Teresa presents her beautiful analogy of the silkworm. This illustrates how a person can make himself or herself disposable to

God so that he may reside and work freely in the heart. Teresa was fascinated and awestruck by the way silk came into being. She was mystified by the way a worm crawling slowly could change into a butterfly flying freely. She explained how the young silkworms nourish themselves by eating mulberry leaves. When they reach a certain stage, the silkworms attach themselves to the twigs of the mulberry bush and begin to spin their cocoons. They spin these cocoons all around themselves. First there is a thin layer of loosely-woven thread, then the layers increase until the silkworm is completely encapsulated in a thick, white cocoon. Inside the cocoon, the worm is transformed into a lovely butterfly. The butterfly emerges from the cocoon and flutters around. The worm has undergone a complete metamorphosis unseen by anyone save God.

The silkworm represents our pilgrim within the first three mansions. There is extensive growth and development through God's graces and one's own efforts. The cocoon represents God, and soon a pilgrim's life becomes hidden with Christ in God inside the fourth mansion. The pilgrim builds the cocoon by eliminating elements of self that detract from God's love and adding elements that enhance his love. When our pilgrim becomes metamorphosed, he or she becomes so filled with Christ that the transformation experienced internally is greater than the external change of the butterfly. The transformation is completed through the prayer of union. One breaks out from the closed darkness of the cocoon freely, radiating God to all.

Teresa said that the longest time the prayer of union lasts is thirty minutes. This time period is much less than the time it takes for a silkworm to change into a butterfly. On the other hand, the internal change within the person is much greater in content and in complexity than the external change of the butterfly. After the transformation takes place our pilgrim desires and strives for nothing outside of Jesus. Since one has been filled with God, one has a consuming drive to live as an extension of his love.

The peace in the fifth mansion is very deep and so are the trials. Both internal and external trials may be suffered in abundance. Most of the time this is accomplished with joyful abandonment, since God has been so deeply experienced. Frequently pain is felt because there is a firm alliance with God. It happens when one sees that others are offending God. The pain is profound owing to an intimate feeling of brotherly love for all members of the mystical body. Any fracture, be it simple or complex, within the mystical body is deeply felt. Our pilgrim has come to be so surrendered in God that there is a deep sharing in the pain that comes through those who do not direct their choices toward love. Our pilgrim shares in the passionate love that God extends to all.

Teresa again shows her concern for a pilgrim on the journey and cautions him or her to continually strive forward in the spiritual life even in this mansion. There is no lying back and taking it easy. This thought can be projected into all other developmental areas of life. A halt along the spiritual path, with a subsequent halt in self-knowledge, may cause one to become negligent. If a firm hold on the self-discipline within prayer is relaxed, an individual can slide down into the lower mansions almost as rapidly as a firefighter slides down a fire pole.

A pilgrim in the fifth mansion is continuously striving to lead a sound Christian life. A sincerity about living is picked up by others even if the pilgrim is void of consolations or delights. The pilgrim radiates the love of God during emptiness and speaks of this love freely even though he or she feels bereft of him.

Teresa emphasizes in the fifth mansion that the prayer of union experienced here is not the only way in which union can be obtained with God. For the majority of us, union with God is accomplished by honestly working at freely uniting our own will with God's will. When this takes place, we need not care at all about the spiritual delights that flow from the prayer of union. In fact, the most favorable expression of the two unions is the union of wills. If this state is reached, we live the ideals and values of the gospel in any given situation. We also enjoy a tranquility that supersedes any adverse event that may befall us. This is not to say that we will not be affected by the event itself. It is just to say that the event will not disturb us at our deepest center. The tranquility is located at the still center of our being. Although the varying difficult events of our lives may cause us to react with sorrow, stress, depression, anxiety, or any other negative response, these reactions will not penetrate our inner tranquility. We react emotionally to different circumstances. Yet these positive or negative responses do not upset the tranquility deep inside. Sometimes, when we are experiencing very difficult times, tranquility is not felt. It is as if it were lost. This can occur through a heartbreaking experience, a change that alters familiar routine, a loss of control or a critical injury. In these and other similar situations, tranquility seems nonexistent, nonsupportive, and it does not even seem as if it will ever return. With the passing of time, it resurfaces. It is through these events that we become more holy, and holiness walks with humanness. Both require vulnerability. Tranquility may be identified with the water at the bottom of a very deep ocean. The movement and temperature of this water remains constant no matter how much the water on the surface changes. Placid seas or violent, raging waves, the interior depths remain calm and still. The storms of our difficult experiences become calm as we see them in the light of the gospel and look for the good that they may hold.

The two main roads that lead to the perfection which God is asking of us, that will eventually result in the union of wills, are well known to all. Travel along these roads is based on the living out of the two commandments of love: love God and love others. By observing them, we are doing all we can to facilitate fusing our own will with God's will. Strong indications are recognizable in showing our love for God. Yet, they only become legitimate if we have the ability to love others. The more advanced we are in loving others, the more advanced we will be in loving God. Although our love can fall short of what we desire it to be, we learn to love the best we can each moment of each day.

It is important, Teresa declares, to walk carefully along the way in which one chooses to love others. Love does not show itself through big plans, wonderful events, or flamboyant and fabulous activities that a person may organize and implement for others. Love shows itself in little, insignificant things. An unexpected visit, a "thinking of you" card sent to celebrate no special occasion, a kind word, a considerate deed, a surprise phone call, all are small but meaningful signs of love. These little things show love through their spontaneous significance. They are not a part of the ordinary, routine day. They are not a function within a person's job or vocation. They are not expected. The giver made time to send or give a special sign of joy to the receiver.

We love others when we show care and concern for them, see their needs, and share what we have with them. Our unobtrusive, empathic responses are given gratuitously. They are not enmeshed with concerns about doing good, cultivating virtue, or affectionate feelings. Teresa was dead set against big things people did in order to prove to the world that they loved God and everyone else. She disapproved of the conduct of those who proved their love by heroic acts that caused much attention, of those who sought to be publicly insulted for God, and of those who based their love on their overactive imaginations. She had a distaste for pious ninnies, phonies, Pollyannas who manifested pseudo enthusiasm, sour-faced saints, those who continually smiled and spoke with a sugary sweetness, and Christians, especially those in Church-related careers, who considered themselves to be highly favored, privileged, chosen ones of God. Oh yes, and there are also those who go about with the look of perpetual martyrdom. Most of Teresa's unfavorite people would have difficulty in authentically living out Jesus' words about love.

Teresa recognized the delicate balance between loving God and loving others. One could not exist in a salubrious state without the other. Teresa frowned on those who preferred to stay in the chapel and pray—not daring to move an eyelid lest they lose their spiritual delights or lose their recollected state while waiting for them—when there were sick people to visit at home or nearby. These Pious Paulas or Prayerful Peters would cause Teresa to swing into action. We can visualize her marching into the chapel and picking up these culprits by the scruff of their necks. She would tell them, strongly and distinctly, that it is God's will for them to visit the sick. This takes priority over dawdling in prayerful self-indulgence. They would serve God better by plumping the pillow of the sick person, or straightening out the blankets, or placing some pretty flowers in the room, or just being present and listening. Such is the way of loving and giving happiness. Remaining in the chapel is a concentration on their own happiness.

While we are on the subject of staying overtime in the chapel, it might be well to mention one other danger. Self-indulgent prayer may lead to inappropriate personal introspection. Here the mind dwells on fanciful exercises that build false muscle around a wounded ego. One dwells on self and fails in love of God and others. Authentic personal introspection centers on one's relationship with God. This may take place at the examen before night prayer. Examen is a time set apart to recall one's thoughts, words and actions during the day and to ask oneself some pertinent questions. What failings need to be overcome? What virtues need to be cultivated? What graces are gratefully received and given? Personal introspection has its time and place, but it is not in prayer, and it needs to be watched for within prayer. If we pray for a strong love for others, and are responsive to the graces God gives, then the graces lead to a strong love of God. Sometimes we find that we must force our will to be loving, kind and respectful to others. It may appear as if we are fighting through our own resistance to do this. When these occasions happen, our introspection, if it is centered on how God sees us, will tell us to strive to rise above the walls of negativism we feel for others. A synergistic power to help with the rising would be to think of Jesus' words which state that when we do good things to others, we do good things to him. Love calls us to believe the best and hold on to the positive in others.

Teresa warns us that we should not feel spiritually secure even in this mansion. She recounts the story of Judas. He was one of the chosen twelve and lived in close union with Jesus. In this mansion we may turn away from God through little things that are colored as good. We may put too much time and effort in little tasks thus over-emphasizing their importance in the scheme of daily duties. In this situation unimportant tasks take precedence over important tasks, and this would disturb the ebb and flow of getting the things done that need to be done during the day. Opportunities that pull us away from God still call with phrases such as "No one will know," or "Just this once," or "Everyone does it."

Carmelite integration

When a person studies the events within a typical Teresian Carmelite day, that person notices there is a balancing and a counter-balancing that keeps the Carmelite on an even keel. There are times for solitude and sharing; silence and communication; prayer and work; and study and recreation. These external balancings were purposefully set down by Teresa in order that her followers would not over-emphasize one particular aspect of their day and fall into wrack and ruin by channeling all their energies into that one event.

In the fifth mansion, we sense a greater internal balancing taking place within our lives. The two balance beams that keep things synchronized, usually with some healthy tension, are well known by now. They are humility and self-discipline. Humility continues to transform through truth. The self-discipline that braced prayer during arid times has extended itself to other areas. Our balancing has become a major thrust in delaying gratification, yet there remains a joy and spontaneity that enhance our daily communications and actions with others. We are aware of our boundaries and limits, yet we remain flexible and adaptable. The more we have emptied ourselves of self, the more we are able to recognize the value of others. The more we live in love with prayer and faith, the deeper our level of personal sharing becomes. We have learned to recognize our own emotions and what they are saying, yet our strong emotions do not interfere with, nor are they the total bases for, our judgments. There is a recognition and acceptance of our personality traits, and there is an awareness that some traits may be abrasive if they become domineering in conversations or in personal relationships. There is the ability to enjoy laughter and the ability to appreciate the tears of someone who is hurting. We are slowly able to let go of things that do not mirror Christ and work toward a continual integration of new information that enlarges our understanding and reality of Christ. We are able to sincerely rejoice in the successes of others and sincerely respond with empathy to the broken dreams of others. We have experienced, or are experiencing, personal pain, yet the pain is enveloped in joy. There is a sustaining balance between our active lives and our contemplative lives.

Of course this balancing is to be watched very carefully and guarded so there is no sliding off the beams. There is no assurance of a continual state of equilibrium here or onward into future mansions. To maintain an equal symmetry will take work and a never-ending stringent evaluation of self. To be open to change toward the good is to be willing to go through personal pain. It is not easy to welcome constructive criticism from ourselves or others. It requires courage to honestly face up to our thoughts and feelings and convey them truthfully to others. Once we have torn down our walls of self-protection, it takes continual work to keep them down. We can easily avoid deep introspection by slipping back into life in the fast lane where overt busyness covers a multitude of confrontations. We can live our whole lives functioning well in our particular roles and being busy with many things. Is this experiencing life at the deepest and richest center? If we would suddenly lose all roles, and have no duties or schedules, how would we define ourselves as persons?

Self-knowledge is often avoided or limited when it is painful. A few common avoidance techniques are known to us all. One is continual involvement in a constant stream of activities that "must" be done. Here is a cover that protects one from pain. "I do not have the time" is often an excellent excuse for avoiding a deep search into the painful areas of self. Another technique is not accepting the responsibility for the problem that causes the pain. Denial is often expressed as: "That is not my fault" or "That is not my problem," or through "spiritualizing" one's weaknesses. This technique distances and divorces a person from the painful situation. A last common technique is placing the pain on the shelf with an individual's idealized self. In this way he or she can never connect with the pain because it cannot be reached. It is here where one hears the "I should" or "I should not" or "I ought to."

In all these cases, the pain that would enlighten a person and cause him or her to go forward in self-knowledge is blocked or avoided. Self-discipline is out of balance through a lack of courage, a personal weakness. If discipline was in balance, it would give an individual strength to face the pain, work with it, integrate it, and then journey on. One would also gain strength to continue to search and risk.

One prerequisite is needed before a person is able to empty self in order to be available to others. The self can empty only if there is a sound and wholesome self-image to sustain the giving quality involved here. An individual gives strength and comfort to others when he or she maintains a respect and love for self as an extension of God's image. One may visualize self as a glass brimming over with water. The glass must be full of water before the water is able to run over and refresh whatever it contacts. So should a person be filled with a healthy, stable, well-integrated self-image before he or she can be of service to others. There is danger in living for others if one has a poor self-image. An individual cannot sincerely care for others unless he or she has a positive love for self. This includes the capacity for both autonomy and intimacy and knowing and respecting one's limits. One can become so tied up with the problems of others that one becomes drained of selfhood, and eventually self-destruction takes place. A person can become so de-energized by the problems of others that he or she ends up living a minimal existence. Some rivers in Arizona are very wide and very shallow. If people were like these rivers they would spread themselves very thin with their many activities and neglect the rich, deep journey to Love within. An over extension in the problems of others may lead to a love that is self-destructive.

People cannot give strength, support and courage to others unless they are secure and comfortable with their internal and external selves. People can extend their limits in a reasonable way for this is the challenge of love, but to extend them to the point of ultimate oblivion is complete foolishness.

In maintaining the balance between the emptying of the false self and the giving to others, it is necessary to identify attention-getting behaviors that may be detrimental within a helping relationship. These attention-getting behaviors draw attention away from the others and on to the self. A few examples will be given and they relate to the absence of attentive listening.

There is the recounting of events that can affirm a person's own self-worth. When the other is sharing an accomplishment, the response is a similar accomplishment that was achieved some years back. A more appropriate response would be to extend one's congratulations, honest praise, and sincere best wishes. When the other is relating a troublesome event, it would be beneficial to restate the event and confirm the feelings associated with it rather than relating a similar troublesome incident that is preceded with "When I was young," or "When I was a novice" or "I remember the time when." An individual is so accustomed to using these familiar phrases that it is natural to revert to them in a helping relationship. However, it should be realized that such responses deal with times that are past within a person's life. The solution that solved the problem then may not fit into the problem of today. This is not living in the present here and now and focusing on the problem of the other. On occasion, such stories are good to comfort and console the other, but if they are used repeatedly, they indicate that there is no real interest in the other person as a unique individual. It is difficult to keep one's thoughts concentrated on the other person and his or her interests, problems, stories, plans, and points of view. This involves attention, effort, concentration and love. It means listening to what the person is saying, how he or she is saying it, the thoughts and feelings behind the words said, and observing nonverbal communication. This is the only way that true concern for the other is expressed, and it goes hand in hand with the emptying of self.

One should not become terribly shaken if one finds one is continually jumping into a conversation with stories about self to share. A person should try to be aware of how often this is done and decrease his or her stories if they are over fifty percent in a dyadic encounter. If a person feels that he or she may have tendencies toward dominating a conversation, the person may want to make mental notes of how often the pronouns I, me, or my are used during the conversation. One may also desire to reflect upon this old English saying: "A wise old owl sat in an oak. The more he heard, the less he spoke. The less he spoke, the more he heard. Why can't we all be like that bird?"

It is true that the giving up of self is a gradual and a never-ending process that began early on in the first mansion and will continue until one's dying day. It is a rocky road full of starts, stops and deviations. The key to continual growth is patience with self and kind firmness in confronting the self with the ever-burning honesty of self-knowledge. Here in the fifth mansion the art of listening has become refined, cultivated and sophisticated through authentic listening to God. Listening to others has also shown similar growth patterns. As our listening skills continually sharpen, our sensitivity to self and the others improves. The more we are attentive to the problems and cares of others, the more we learn about ourselves. This gives rise to a more refined self-evaluation and an improvement in communication skills with others.

Reflecting again on helping relationships, we can now see that the helper takes a low-key approach and basically listens. When necessary, feedback is given to the other but rarely in an advice-giving contest. Advice can be given occasionally when there is a genuine need for it. The listening evokes love of the other when it is nonjudgmental and accepting of the other person as he or she is here and now. When there is a genuine love for the other, the distinction between the self and the other is always maintained. It is possible that a person can use others for his or her own emotional needs, personal desires, or interpretation of what the other should be. A person desires the other to be a carbon copy of his or her own thoughts and feelings or hopes and dreams. This is seeing the other as an extension of the self rather than seeing the other as a unique individual. The extension of self shows a using of the other for one's own purposes. It is sometimes seen in relationships between spouses, parent and child, employer and employee, or superior and members of a community. This is not respecting the other as an independent person in his or her own right. Rather, it is a narcissistic object choice. To sculpture others into one's own image is reserved for God alone.

Now we come to the balancing of joy in pain. Herein lies a changing of focus. Traditionally Catholics have called much attention to Jesus in his passion and agony on the cross. Attention to Jesus' interior joy that resulted from doing the Father's will was moderate. Jesus did not want to experience pain. None of us, if we are honest, want to experience pain. To say yes or no to a particular vocation in life is a choice made by the individual. For Jesus, and for many of us, the presence of pain does not allow for a choice. However, in union with Jesus we try to accept our pain, in a positive way, if the pain remains after all reasonable forms of treatment have been exhausted and sufficient prayers for God's will to be done have been said. Although we live in hope, if the pain remains, we cannot choose to change our particular brand of pain or the degree in which the pain hurts. Jesus did not look at his pain as how he could "suffer" for his Father. There was no indication that the more he "suffered" the better he would fulfill his Father's mission. Jesus accepted the type of pain he had with resignation because it was his Father's plan for him. It must have been extremely difficult for Jesus to know the way he was going to die. The sufferings Jesus bore during his life were a consequence of the evils of humankind. Jesus followed his Father's will when he accepted the events in his life with love and trust. His pain did not cause him to complain or to wail and bemoan his fate. Jesus did not pray for more or less pain. Jesus' cry to his Father in the garden was one of terror, bewilderment and sorrow. Yet, he looked to his Father with ultimate trust and listened to him from the depths of his heart. Jesus' prayer at Gethsemane did not center so much on his own personal agony but on the messianic agony of the world. The total reality of Jesus' life on earth was marked by his unwavering and intense love, peace, joy and forgiveness of others.

To embrace pain joyfully and eventually integrate it so that it is not thought of as an element of suffering is to open ourselves up to be called to serve in a way that may require more pain. By acknowledging the reality of our own pain, yet not becoming a product of it, we may become more open and aware of the pain of others even if it is held in secret, for there are many who are laughing on the outside while crying on the inside. Their brave smiles cover the silent tears of their hidden pain. Our pain grafts us into the wounded heart of Christ. We learn to share the vulnerability that comes from our pain with others. His heart is where our bleeding hurts are healed. Many times we may be healed through a spiritual healing while our pain continues. New life emerges from our healing. It is a life which loves and shares pain at the risk of being rejected or having our wounds reopened. In a physical context pain can be a liberating agent which frees us toward activities that may flow into contemplation. For people who have restrictions of their neuromuscular systems, there may be an inability to participate in active sports, so the time that could be channeled into sports events may now be channeled into developing artistic or other creative talents. Frequently those with visible signs of a physical disability are less handicapped than those who are in a normal state of physical well-being, but are trapped in their own egoisms. A crutch or a wheelchair is only a means to enhance external mobility. What about internal mobility? Often it becomes constricted or totally occluded by exaggerations, fear of involvement, generalizations, hate, hostility, indifference, narrow-mindedness, negativisms, obsessions with power, pessimism, prejudices, rash judgments, resentments, righteousness, stereotyping or timidity. What is more restricting to self-knowledge here? Internal mobility. Who is really handicapped? Self-knowledge whispers, "Each one of us."

The above restrictions on mind mobility are not part of the pain that is balanced in joy. Most of them are learned behaviors. These behavioral traits are indigenous to the early stages of spiritual development. It appears that they are all underlined by laziness. There can be no growth or change if no effort is exerted toward growth or change. These elements are all within us in varying degrees, but they should diminish as we journey forward in the spiritual life. These behavioral traits are like a deadly plaque that, if not arrested, will slowly build and choke off the blood supply that sustains life. They produce a tunnel vision which sets many limits on our perception of reality. The spiritual journey is one that flows out of a microcosmic view of reality toward and into a macrocosmic perspective. In order for this to be accomplished, we put preventative measures into practice by being aware of the signs which indicate that the behaviors of mind immobility are present. Then we set about to destroy them as soon as possible. The path of prayer requires a contradiction of these immobilizers of the mind. Growth in prayer emphasizes the positive behaviors that oppose negative and restrictive behaviors.

To avoid pain in whatever context it comes is to avoid life. Pain will be risked in trusting others, loving others, and in moving ahead in all areas of life. Growth involves change, change involves risk, risk involves pain, and pain is enveloped in joy. Growing, as indicated within the fourth mansion, requires constant leaps into the unknown. We never cease to grow as long as there are small and sometimes large opportunities in which we can risk to do things differently. As long as the difference is directed toward love, we may be assured that we are becoming stronger in God.

In seeking the balance between the active life and the contemplative life, a person experiences a creative tension. There is the "outward pull" of becoming through activities and a "waiting for" in being through contemplation. In the active life a person gratefully throws out all nonessentials. Again, this requires an honest appraisal of what an individual needs and what he or she wants. When the majority of one's wants are discarded, there may be more free time available. If the trivia and incidentals of life are let go, then a person can take the time to learn how to do new things. One would be able to solve simple problems instead of shrugging them off through ignorance. If a simple task was necessary to fix the car, plumbing or television, how gratifying it would be, in more ways than one, to take the time to learn how to fix it rather than having to call the repair person. Such small challenges keep a person's perception of reality ever growing. Time may also be taken to be still. In stillness one becomes patient and receptive to the silent, timeless prayer of contemplation.

The central criteria needed to avoid trouble in the fifth mansion is the willingness to confront a balancing problem early. In doing so we will pull the problem out of its roots before it gets a chance to grow. This resembles pulling out a tiny weed in a lovely garden before the weed gets bigger. A person exercises the discipline of responsibility when he or she faces a problem at first notice and resolves it. The individual is dealing with the problem before it gets out of hand. If we deny the existence of the problem after our initial contact with it, the problem grows and the solution will come through circumstance. This resembles the tiny weed which has now grown. The weed has taken over the garden and has killed all the beautiful flowers in it. It is now so grotesque and so gigantic that it is invading all aspects of the property. The circumstance requires that the owner had better get busy with an axe or a chain saw before complete invasion forces him to move off his land.

It is not difficult to see that each internal balancing mentioned is manifested through some external expression. Each individual expression and all expressions collectively give witness to others that the pilgrim is living Jesus. The pilgrim's love radiates incarnate Love. The pilgrim's eyes see with the vision of the Messiah. The pilgrim's thoughts parallel the thoughts of Christ. The pilgrim's feet walk the path the Savior took on earth, and the pilgrim seeks to pray and love with the intensity of Jesus in his sacred humanity.

The importance of simplicity

In the fifth mansion Teresa again affirms our pilgrims. They need not be troubled if they do not receive spiritual delights from God. Spiritual delights and the persons who receive them should not concern our pilgrims. Teresa said that there is no reason for the pilgrims to meddle in these matters. Here she emphasizes that the way to praise and serve God is through humility and simplicity of heart. Through simplicity, the pilgrims find value in the ordinary.

What are the facets of simplicity? Does it describe a dearth of intelligence? No. Is it a means by which we take the back seat and just go along for the ride by avoiding decisions that involve risk along the road of life? No. Does a major element of simplicity indicate that we place responsibility for our own actions and behaviors on another person or thing? No. Does simplicity mean living the easy life, out in the country, sitting in a rocker with our feet propped up on a table? No. Is it not seeking a solution when there are no set solutions? No. Is it an inhibitor that prevents us from going beyond our own needs in order to meet the needs of another? No. All these facets of simplicity are quite off the track. Simplicity, in the spiritual sense and in this mansion, is an external expression of an internal reality. A simplicity of heart is manifested by a naturalness, a gentleness, and a serenity which are charming to behold in an individual. It also includes an unpretentiousness, a veraciousness, a straightforwardness, an unassuming nature and a serendipity. Serendipity is the gift of simplicity which finds value and agreement in things that are not sought after or planned. This could connect very well with seeing everything as a grace.

Simplicity is shown in a way of life that is uncluttered by ornaments, gimmicks, gadgets, fads, incidentals, useless cares, fancy prayers, compulsive talk, and preoccupations. Simplicity was humbly and peacefully lived by Mary. In her ponderings she showed us interior simplicity of the heart. Simplicity, as an internal reality, bases its attention lovingly on the God within. Slowly it evolves into a major charism of an individual's external life style. There is, then, a liberation from extravagance, status, possessions, or control of things and/or people. Freedom comes through focusing in on the divine center. It is gradually learned that life can be lived profoundly without many things. When that point is reached, there is an internal and external balancing of simplicity. This is why simplicity is presented here in the fifth mansion. Simplicity is built on this synchronized balance. If the balance is not maintained from within and does not flow out from a person's centering on God, then simplicity could be taken out of its context in the spiritual life and used to support one's negative egoisms. Simplicity deepens the essentials of the spiritual journey and drops the unnecessary accidentals and superfluous activities that may have accumulated along one's road of life.

The freedom to receive all things as gifts that come from God and to put them to good use and not to keep them for oneself is a mature expression of simplicity. These gifts are freely shared with others. As one receives from God, one also gives to him. Giving is done peacefully and simply, as Teresa teaches, through concentrating on and offering the duty of the moment no matter what that duty may be. Within the Carmelite charism this is a person's gift offering of love and service to God. When one gives these simple gifts, he or she finds sanctity in the task at hand, fidelity to little things and reverence for the commonplace.

All these words about simplicity are good, but how can our pilgrims simplify their lives in this incredibly busy, noisy, technological world? A few necessities of life will be presented with an attempt to illustrate how simplicity might be integrated into them. Our pilgrims may want to pick a few suggestions and blend them into their own activities of daily living.

Food: Prepare meals according to their nutritional value, keeping in mind the four food groups rather than preparation according to likes or dislikes. Use simple recipes. That is, those recipes that call for less than ten ingredients, have easy instructions to follow, and do not take a lengthy amount of time to prepare. Eat raw fruits and vegetables to satisfy the mid-meal munchies. Be aware of and limit your intake or avoid any food or drink that can become addictive (coffee, tea, carbonated beverages, alcohol, sweets). It may be best to keep nonessential addictive items out of the house. Be aware of other items that can become addictive such as the radio, television, telephone, work, sleep, et cetera. Meal plan simply and table set according to need rather than formalities. Try to avoid foods with animal fat, chemicals and other additives. After you have sat down at the table, and before you have begun to eat, pause, relax, and clear the mind of the tensions and troubles of the day. Eat in moderation with a calm, relaxed attitude. Chew thoroughly, eat slowly, using the amount of time that is comfortable for your body. All these factors aid in your digestion. Substitute nuts, raisins, and other natural foods for foods with a high sugar content. Leave the table before you are full. Oh yes, and do not forget cooking prayers and eating prayers.

Clothing: In order to minimize the possibility of skin irritations do not use clothing that binds, chafes, or restricts movements in any way. Choose clothing that feels good. You should feel comfortable with the style, color, fit and how the material feels against the skin. Step out of the fashion race and buy clothes only when the old ones are worn out. Purchase clothes for their practical use rather than for show. Look for clothes that are at least fifty percent cotton, wool or silk. Man-made fibers often do not let air circulate through them nor are they absorbent. The fibers are nonporous and perspiration and body heat are held in causing the skin to over-heat and disrupt normal skin temperature. If you make your own clothes, use simple patterns. Frills, gathers, pleats, and other complexities require more time at the ironing board. To eliminate ironing altogether, use wash and wear materials. Wash your clothes and yourself using non-irritating, pure soap. Clothing is like a second skin. Choose your clothes to match the season.

Work: Teresa notes that tasks are done with simplicity if they are performed cheerfully, carefully and doused with generous amounts of joyful goodwill. For necessary but unpleasant tasks, try to find ways to make them enjoyable. You may turn your attention to a part of the task that looks and feels good. For instance, when washing the dishes, look at the whiteness of the soap bubbles and feel the warm water against your skin. The effervescent Mary Poppins had something to say here: "In every job that must be done, there is an element of fun." Granted, sometimes you must really look for it, but it is there. Joy can be found when task accomplishment gives order and beauty to a home. If you feel tense before beginning a task, do some relaxation exercises. Plan ahead. Collect all items needed before beginning a task and arrange them in order of use. Try and find a quiet place to work. Loud noise, high levels of activity, noxious odors, and bright or dim light all deplete energy. Eliminate unnecessary clutter on shelves and in the working area. Set up the work area to permit a coordinated flow of activity (preparation, task performance, clean up). Maintain good posture during the task. Try to keep your mind free from worry and complaints so that you are able to concentrate on the task and work on it with love. Wear comfortable clothes and make sure there is proper ventilation. Remember necessary and precautionary safety rules. Usually, an easier or better way may be found to complete a task, if the task takes too long, makes you tired or uses up too much energy. When purchasing items for a task, buy things for their purposeful usefulness rather than for status or because the item is the new and improved model. Think twice about fad gadgetry. Is this item really better than the old stand-by? Does it really save time and energy? When purchasing expensive items, extreme caution should precede going into debt. Installment plans can lead to ruin. A good rule to live by is: do not buy what you do not need or will not use. Junk drawers, shelves and closets may be cluttered with unnecessary items. If these items have not been used within the year, or if there are duplicates, you should think about giving them away. Perhaps some other person would benefit from them. You should discard anything that is broken beyond repair, unsafe, useless, inoperable or a cause for danger or undue worry.

Recreation: To find leisure time activities that are simple is to bring forth a gaiety and charm that springs from the wonder of the simple gifts of God. Look at the magical, myriad beauty of nature when walking or jogging. Feel the cool ocean as it rushes over your feet at the shore. Smell the aroma of freshly baked bread, cut grass, or rain in the woods. Hear the variants of song not only from birds but from all of God's critters. Experience the warm and tender touch of a loved one. Focus in on the ongoing, yet unseen, physical gifts that work quietly, smoothly and unceasingly to sustain life. Pay attention to the ongoing mental gifts that give the power to think, dream, understand, probe, muse, remember, love and care. All speak so profoundly of God's goodness in his creation. What are some suggestions that show simplicity in leisure? If you are going to some recreational area that is within walking or biking distance, do not use the car. Visit the beach, library, museum, park, forest, zoo or any other place that does not require purchasing in order to enjoy. Exercise every day and view it as a pleasure rather than a chore. Exercise out of doors in the sunshine and fresh air if possible. You need not be a member of a health spa or own expensive exercise equipment to stay in shape. Use exercise as a daily vacation from the pressures, tensions and duties of your daily routine. Locate and maintain a personal, peaceful place in your soul where you are free from worrisome or negative thoughts or feelings. Avoid organizations, groups, social functions, or activities that support the exploitation or oppression of others.

An important and delightful area in leisure time activities that speak of simplicity, is the ability to play. Play is characterized by fun and spontaneity and a heart full of joy. It keeps an individual in touch with the gaiety of childhood. A person retains a childlike wonder if he or she maintains the ability to play. This is not lost by age or maturity. The only thing that can erode playfulness into a state of nonexistence is a snootiness that smothers one's humor, mischievousness, naturalness, imagination, openness to be teased, or appreciation for the amusing qualities of life. Play is delighted in for itself alone. There is wonderment at and absorption in a common event that makes the commonplace magical. There are no results and no goals to meet. Play brings out a unique inner freedom that flows into the joyful experience of being in the present moment. Play is anything that revitalizes through its invitation to be carefree, lithesome and imaginatively alert to the here and now. There is an active participation with joyful abandon. One does not care what the others may think. Go ahead!! Beat someone at jacks. Jump in the hopscotch squares. Stomp in the rain puddles. Boogie to some hot rock music. Create a unique self portrait through finger painting. Bake some chewy, gooey cookies. Blow bubbles. Fly a kite and send a message to it in a secret code. Climb a tree. Watch a funny cartoon. Listen to the ocean in a sea shell. Look for the animals in the clouds. Read a fairy tale. Find Teddy Bear and give him a hug. Almost everyone should have a Teddy, for this bear will keep his owner young at heart!

Within one's interpersonal relationships in the fifth mansion, a kindred spirit continues to develop. A union and bonding with this person goes beyond time and space. The abiding warmth of this friendship often lifts an individual from the doldrums of apathy, despair, dejection and indifference. Even when the other is not physically present, the person feels the presence of the other. In times of joys and sorrows and in the ordinary humdrum days, the other is present inside the heart in a loving spiritual way. This is such a loving bond that there is a union of two hearts which beats as one heart, and one love overflows so that the person is able to love others in a more sincere way. There is a great love and an in-depth sharing with the soul friend. The desires of the heart are exchanged. A loving openness to the serious and a delight in sharing little things add depth and sparkle to the day. A comical phrase, a song sung together, skipping stones over a lake, or giving the other a flower for no particular reason, all bring a delicious spontaneity that binds with love. Whether solemn or cheerful, sharings with the soul friend are directed toward growth in love, support and mutual encouragement. The friend is cherished, yet never ceases to be an unfathomable mystery.

In humility the pilgrim remembers daily that without God he or she is lost. It is God who sustains and maintains things in their proper order. An individual depends on God and his love and gives expression of this love by considering himself or herself the least important of all. Love grounded in humility is never idle, for it impels one to constantly place others first. Life grounded in humility is not intense or urgent. Humility is truth and accepts all gifts as coming from God. It does not swagger in successes, resent limitations or grovel in failures. Humility is a homespun reality of the heart which finds happiness in serving others. There is a deep appreciation of human life that sees all people as equal in importance regardless of who they are. Within the individual pilgrim, Martha and Mary have fused together as one. The pilgrim is ever in the presence of God and serving others without the customary hustle and bustle that was previously known. Through a faithful performance of ordinary tasks the pilgrim experiences a new sense of liberation because slavery to earthly pursuits and possessions no longer exist. There will be falls, blind spots, and flaws, but the pilgrim is now in full spiritual maturity and will be able to confront these things because the heart of the pilgrim is meshed within God's indwelling presence.

Sixth Mansion

MYSTICAL EXPERIENCES
AND INTERIOR DESERT

Our sixth mansion may be viewed as the mansion of the surrendered heart. The journey of the heart to total surrender to God is a long journey, therefore this mansion is very large. It is of a substantial size because many extraordinary mystical experiences may happen here. They are combined with many trials. Teresa explains them in detail in the eleven chapters which she devotes to this mansion. The sixth mansion can be seen as a connecting force that unites the first mystical outpourings of God's love in the fifth mansion with the transformation of that love in the seventh mansion. The sixth mansion is a continuation of the prayer of union which embodies that love, and now it is experienced more deeply. This loving union will reach perfection in the mansion that is to come.

Many of our pilgrims are inquisitive by nature, and it seems as if they have been moved by that most interesting phrase "extraordinary mystical experience." In order to subdue their inquisitive longings, we shall present this element of the sixth mansion first.

In the sixth mansion there is a strong sense of belonging to God that is experienced with a ferocious reality. God belongs to the pilgrim and the pilgrim belongs to God through a total surrender and abandonment of the pilgrim's heart to God. The essence of belonging transpires by enigmatic ways which the pilgrim does not understand. It proceeds from the unionization of the deepest part of the pilgrim's spirit and the deepest nature of God. The experiences that flow from this belonging are very different from the spiritual delights. These experiences may be categorized under the broad heading of "extraordinary mystical experiences." The unifying characteristics are: They are very intense. They last for a longer period of time than the spiritual delights. They combine deep spiritual pain with deep spiritual pleasure. Extraordinary mystical experiences are much more rigorous than delights. It is as if one has become wounded by love. The depth and duration of these wounds depend on how God wishes to communicate them. Because these wounds are so filled with a radical spiritual energy, they never last long. In this context the use of the term "wound" does not mean a grisly break in the skin with blood flowing out of it. It does mean any extraordinary mystical experience which combines the pain and pleasure found within a high level spiritual union. This might be comparable to a feeling that a person has if he or she is being consumed internally by fire. An excellent visual expression of one of these experiences is found in Bernini's statue of Teresa in ecstasy that stands in Rome. Here he is giving expression to one form of her mystical experiences.

There are several kinds of extraordinary mystical experiences. The first experience Teresa describes is a locution. A locution is an inner mystical communication that comes from God and is received by the pilgrim through the sense of hearing, the intellect, or the imagination. Teresa describes well how our pilgrim may be deceived by pseudo locutions. She gives them pointers to indicate the true source of these locutions. Her words of wisdom here can very well be extended to any other phenomena that fall within the realm of extraordinary mystical experiences.

If the locutions come from God, Teresa's primary concern is that the pilgrim must not think himself or herself better for having experienced them. Then she gives us the signs that indicate when locutions are from God.

First: The locutions seem very powerful, and they leave the pilgrim with a great peace that overrides all adversity that he or she may experience because of the locutions. Second: There is a readiness to praise and love God that is surrounded by a great quiet and a beauty filled recollection. Third: The context of the locution remains in one's memory for a long period of time, and sometimes it is never forgotten. The certitude of the contents remains even though a person cannot completely understand it, or doubts from the mind occasionally intimidate it. Fourth: The pilgrim is assured that the locution comes from God despite contradictory statements that come from clergy, religious, and others who say such things are absurd. Fifth: There is a very real knowledge transmitted and, although not completely understood, it changes one's life toward the good. If these locutions are from the evil one, they can be recognized by their lack of coherence or clarity. They cause the pilgrims to be in a confused and tumultuous state that is heightened by anxiety. The external signs that accompany these locutions are all marked by the fact that everything goes against love. There are also musings that the pilgrims are more holy than everyone else around them. These pilgrims consider themselves, secretly of course, to be among the chosen elite of the exalted mystical set.

The locution is only an illusion if it originates from the imagination.

A higher incidence of this type of locution may be found among people who are easily excitable, intense, have over-active imaginations, are gullible, or who follow the suggestions of others easily. Those who are susceptible to frequent states of melancholia may experience this type of locution. Teresa said that no attention should be given to the descriptions of these locutions. The people are to be treated as sick persons and it would be in their best interest to seek professional help.

There are many other manifestations of extraordinary mystical experiences. The ecstasy may resemble a gentle and deep spiritual union accompanied by an out-of-body experience. The rapture is like an ecstasy but is sudden and somewhat violent. There can be no resistance to it. Teresa shares several different types of raptures that can happen in the sixth mansion of the interior castle. The vision is the mystical perception of Jesus, Mary, or any saint as seen by the eye of the intellect or the inner eye. Teresa describes these extraordinary mystical experiences well because they happened to her. Her explanations are colorful, rich, profound, detailed and dramatic. They flow from her own perspective and personality. It is wise to remember that her illustrations are given from the historical and cultural context of the life style in which Teresa was living. Her general knowledge and the knowledge that was available at her time are also important factors to keep in mind when reading Teresa's explanations of the effects that came from the mystical experiences she had. Knowledge concerning the various components of human development was barely in its embryonic stages in her era.

Because God reveals himself to each pilgrim in a different way, it has been decided not to give much coverage to Teresa's personal descriptions of her physical and mental experiences that came through her many mystical encounters. The pilgrim of today may view Teresa's experiences as rather severe in intensity and "way out" as far as the physical manifestations are concerned. If similar experiences are exhibited by a person today, they may receive an entirely different interpretation.

Let us say that one of our meticulous pilgrims enjoys writing and is busy recording his spiritual journey step by step. He is using the *Interior Castle* as a guide and is very diligent in writing down all the extraordinary mystical experiences that happen to him in the sixth mansion. Eventually his spiritual journal is published. Four hundred years have passed, and by Jove, there is still human life present in these United States. However, it is far different from what we know today. A future pilgrim of that era picked up the journal. He found it in a prestigious, old university library and read it with interest. The reader chuckled some, expressed his admiration for the author, and at times thought of the writer as a bit of an odd duck because of the expressions used when relating the extraordinary mystical experiences. Such are the ways of culture, language, history and developmental knowledge as time marches on. Each pilgrim, in whatever time spot he or she is marching, seeks to be an authentic person with an original makeup of gifts, limitations, commonalities that unify and, yes, oddities that diversify.

Teresa tells her pilgrims that they are not to look for the reasons God grants them extraordinary mystical experiences, nor are they to probe into an in-depth understanding of these experiences, for that is impossible. During these experiences God carries the pilgrims off to his land of mystery. Our pilgrims have as much ability to understand what is happening to them as a worm has in understanding what it means to be human. When these overpowering experiences occur, the pilgrims are beside themselves. They are totally suspended in God. It is more intense than anything that has happened before. Because of this intensity, this actual encounter with God does not last long, but the after effects may be felt for several days following the experience.

The prerequisite for these experiences is a strong and sustaining courage. Courage will be tried in more ways than one. There is to be a total and unquestioning faith and confidence in God. The pilgrim lets God be God with no reservations or restrictions, and there is a full surrender to let God do what he wants with the pilgrim. To be carried off by God through one of these extraordinary mystical experiences means that the pilgrim gives up any control, any say so, or any input, in any way, shape or form regarding what will happen.

The understanding that can be obtained from these mystical experiences may be very enlightening, and this puts our pilgrim on guard. Laziness can be found lurking in the sixth mansion. Covered with a mystical blanket it can wrap itself around our pilgrim very easily. How elegant it is to receive knowledge directly from God! How dignified can one get? Our pilgrim has a special resource available to very few. The pilgrim experiences God's love directly from God. Does this mean that the pilgrim ceases to seek knowledge through spiritual books, workshops, conferences and so forth? No. Does this mean that the pilgrim no longer experiences God's love through the eucharistic sacrifice, the sacraments, or scripture? No. A pilgrim is in a sad state if his or her mind conjures up the desire to be singled out because of these mystical experiences. In truth, there is no desire to be special rather than commonplace, or to be set apart rather than run-of-the-mill. If our pilgrim has these musings, the authenticity of the mystical experiences has a right to be questioned. If they are from God, the pilgrim does not view himself or herself as a chosen soul. There is only contentment in being an ordinary Christian and courage that resists laziness every step of the way.

Our pilgrim learns to walk with caution after receiving one or many of these extraordinary mystical experiences. The pilgrim does not feel self-confident because these experiences have been received. One does not speak of these events freely even to learned or very spiritual people. A pilgrim makes haste slowly in finding a confidant with whom these experiences can be shared. When a confidant is found, the individual is able to share quite openly and truthfully. It is known that God does not lead everyone along the same spiritual path. Teresa's path is one among many, so it would be well to have a confidant that is traveling along the same path.

In this mansion Teresa again consoles those of us who do not receive any of these mystical experiences. They are not required for advancement in the spiritual journey, she says soothingly, nor are they signs of approval from God. There are thousands of wholesome, holy pilgrims who have never encountered an extraordinary mystical experience, and there are those who think they have, who are far from holy or wholesome.

Prayer in this mansion is very similar to prayer in the last mansion. The only difference is that there is an intensification within the prayer of union. Prayer consists primarily of active prayer which has become an old, familiar, and loving standby. Passive prayer may be felt at times. Prayer still requires work. A person persists in prayer without expecting any returns. One prays for the glory of God. The pilgrim's prayer life is the primary reality in his or her life. Therefore, the flow from that prayer gives life outside of prayer a vitality and authenticity that meets each new day as a challenge. The pilgrim does not depend on assurance or reassurance that the life he or she is living is worthwhile, meaningful or successful. The pilgrim is not concerned about the value or significance of prayer. One needs no continual reminders that one's prayer is appreciated. The pilgrim may have had some extraordinary mystical experiences, but they have not changed his or her physical makeup. An individual has not sprouted wings, nor has one become a great sage because of these experiences. If a pilgrim has a problem with gross motor coordination before the mystical experience, the problem will probably remain. A person has not turned into a graceful, poised ballerina-like creature through these experiences. Active prayer may be the mainstay of prayer for many years to come. The pilgrim may long for the mystical experiences, but such longings, according to Teresa, are only a waste of time. It would make no sense at this point to sit around with a mind like a blank slate waiting for God to fill it with mystical messages. This is only pride. God will communicate his mystical messages when he pleases. Expecting such things is a refusal to work at prayer. It is also a denial of one's humanness. God gave our pilgrim a brain and he expects it to be used. The prudent pilgrim does not squander away time acting like some high mystic. If a pilgrim dwells on his or her problems in prayer or daydreams about more mystical experiences, Teresa urges this pilgrim to engage in some form of charitable work. When our pilgrim places attention on the task, the problems and daydreams become de-emphasized. Such works may serve as a needed and necessary respite from problematic spiritual ponderings. They will certainly rechannel one's energy into something practical.

Prayer in the sixth mansion may be very delightful and also very loathsome. The loathsome prayer is not lost if one perseveres despite its repulsiveness. Rather, it is a great gain. There is no thought of self here. The pilgrim has let go of any possible rewards and there are no expectations. A person prays and labors because God is God, and oftentimes these valiant efforts are met with inner pain and a feeling of loneliness. Teresa repeats over and over not to let one's heart cling to inner solaces. Her little story about the two military men fits very well here. The pilgrim is no longer a common soldier who demands wages for his work done. Our pilgrim is now a strong officer who gives his services to the king for nothing.

Grace in disguise

Now our pilgrim is beginning to see that the journey in the sixth mansion is not a delight-filled frolic along a high mystical path. The deep loving communications with God are well balanced with hardships and trials, both external and internal, psychological and physical. They are the proving ground that will test our pilgrim's worth. Because this is a high mansion, these difficulties are not viewed in the negative. They are considered as blessings. Of course, the blessings will not be realized upon one's first meeting with a difficulty, but given time they will emerge.

Fortitude is the armor worn by our pilgrim in this mansion, for his or her battle with difficult trials will be easier if this virtue is learned deeply.

These trials and hardships will naturally vary in their degree of difficulty and their number. They will also serve as a mode for cleansing and strengthening the pilgrim.

As the extraordinary mystical experiences can be compared to a fire, so can trials and hardships. Uniting hardships with fire is analogous to the action of flames upon a branch of wood. Some minor hardships are like sparks that just singe the wood. Some trials are like flames that scorch the wood. The more difficult stresses and conflicts resemble the branch when it is repeatedly plunged into the fire. First the fire burns the outer bark of the wood. This dries up and turns to ash exposing the white wood. The fire continues slowly, crumbling the remainder of the branch into its burning embers. The branch is no longer the branch. It is part of the fire. The process of purification takes from the pilgrim all that is not of God and replaces it with a love that is burning for God. This is a continual process. It is not easy because of the pain involved but, in this mansion, it is all endured and offered for love.

Teresa was very diligent in giving her accounts regarding her extraordinary mystical experiences. She did this so that her pilgrims would understand what might happen to them. She continues her thoughtful considerations regarding the trials that lie ahead. She feels it would be very helpful for our pilgrims to know something about what is to come.

We know that extraordinary mystical experiences are not required for a successful journey through the sixth mansion. The trials in this mansion may or may not be related to these experiences. However, the following trial is one that is related.

The pilgrim who sustains these mystical experiences is somewhat set apart. Through these encounters a person is changed, he or she is different. After these mystical experiences have been felt, the pilgrim is left with a mild restlessness. This is an interior hardship. The restlessness is soft and subtle. It is continuous and lies deep in the heart. It is a gentle feeling, a longing to be with God because the tenderness of his love has been personally experienced as if one were in heaven. The pilgrim longs to return to this state. There was a resting in the burning flames of God's love without fear. Now there is a restlessness because the fire is not there in its ferocity. The restlessness may be described as a deep longing to be joined forever to him who is love. The pilgrim does not dwell on this restlessness, nor does it restrict functioning within his or her daily activities. No attention is given to it. Yet, its sensitive presence remains. Our pilgrim finds a deep unification with Augustine's words: "You have made us for yourself O God, and our hearts are restless until they rest in you."

One psychological hardship Teresa mentions is that of misinterpretation. For one reason or another our pilgrim's words or actions have been taken for what they were not meant to be. This has happened to us all, but when it happens regarding phenomena that occur in this mansion, it could be deadly. Misinterpretations may cause friends to turn away, idle gossip to explode into malicious slander, ridicule, scorn, sarcasm, or hostility. These are the products of a negative misinterpretation. Positive misinterpretation can be just as deadly. This may result in undue but lavish praise, honor, compliments, commendations and exaltations. All this adoration is given to the pilgrim, and the pilgrim knows that any good that comes from him or her is given by God. Unwarranted praise is not as difficult to endure as unwarranted condemnation, but it can result in false humility. Teresa suggests that a pilgrim caught in either of these situations pays no attention to the bad or the good that is spoken about him or her. Those people who are quick with praise may also be quick with contempt. The good, if it is authentic, is given back to God in praise. The bad is overlooked by forgiveness from the heart and tender love for the persecutors. In this stage of spiritual development, the pilgrim pays little attention to the approval or disapproval that comes from others.

Our pilgrim experiences interior pain when he or she sees self or others fall away, even in the slightest of degrees, from God's love. It is a sorrowing pain that comes when one sees oneself or another offending God in very little ways. There is the occasional convenient lie. A person finds an easy excuse to get out of doing something. An individual does not speak when a kind word would have brightened the day for another. There is a change in wording of a story or message to give it a different emphasis. It is easy to let the other guy do it. One puts off visiting a shut-in. A harsh word is spoken. There is a small play in dominance within a conversation. A phone call or letter is promised but omitted. There is no follow through on the phrase, "I'll see you soon." Although these incidents are subtle, they are still noticed. Our pilgrim practices inconspicuous and sensible penitential acts to make reparation to God for his or her failings and the failings of others. Our pilgrim desires not to offend God in any way, but being human, there are occasional and sometimes frequent slips.

Our pilgrim may also feel sorrow for a lack of gratefulness toward God for all his gifts. The pilgrim may be lacking in graciousness and generosity toward others too, for he or she sees God's gifts through them. Within this mansion the individual realizes how important it is to thank God for just being God and expressing himself through others. Because our pilgrim is closer to God than ever before, there is a greater sensitivity to his or her own shortcomings. These shortcomings are like superficial cuts that mar the mirror image of God's love that the pilgrim is trying to reflect to others.

The more a pilgrim knows the grandeur of God, the more the distance is felt from him. This is the deepest of interior trials that the pilgrim may experience. This spiritual pain exceeds any other imaginable type of pain. The suffering that results from it is endured willingly. There is joy in this suffering. It is sweet and welcome. One longs to die to be with God, but a pilgrim is content to do as God wishes for this is being obedient to him.

Teresa was well schooled in the art of physical suffering. This was her favored form of trial and a constant companion throughout her religious life. Physical pain shaped and formed this valiant woman, enabling her to follow the path of Jesus with a true fervor. To follow Jesus was Teresa's greatest desire. Her illnesses were heroically borne for the love of God. She is an example for us all. Her pain was very real, yet it did not dominate or interfere with her mission in life. Rather, it refined all qualities of her personality to an exquisite degree. She tells our pilgrims that physical pain can be an interior trial as well as an exterior trial. At times physical pain can be quite severe. The severity affects the mind and the pilgrim just does not know what to do. Times of great confusion during the initial moments of severe pain are not uncommon. Shortly afterwards, proper medical attention is sought out and treatment procedures are initiated. Combined with prayer they bring the mind back from its confused state.

Physical illness or a critical injury becomes an external trial through the attitudes of others. As one example, let us look at a person whose injury has resulted in some type of visible recognition. What goes on within the minds of others when they see this person? To illustrate this point let us look at what is commonly called an attitudinal barrier.

One of our pilgrims in the sixth mansion is a young man. He has a lot of spunk, determination, and realistic goals in life. During his teenage years he sustained a spinal cord injury which left his lower extremities paralyzed. Our pilgrim uses a wheelchair. He is able to perform his self-care and daily living activities by himself. The young man's injury matured and strengthened him. He is now married, has two children, and is a practicing attorney.

Our pilgrim and his family have just moved into a new parish. Four members of the Pious Ladies Society saw our pilgrim at Mass one Sunday. He attended Mass alone because the children had the flu and he was going to babysit while his wife attended a later Mass. Our four pious ladies are middle class, well meaning, and sincere women. However, their contact with anyone in a wheelchair has been only visual. The ladies watched our pilgrim leave church after Mass that Sunday. We can imagine this aggrandized, fabled scene: "Oh, that poor soul," said Mrs. Sadface, "How he has been chosen to suffer for God. He must be very holy." Mrs. Sadface may be an example of pious pity which no one needs. She may assume that all Christians who suffer have a high degree of holiness. This is a pious generalization that is dangerous to make. "Oh, yes," said Mrs. B. Well, "I am so grateful for my health. I can just imagine how horrid it must be to sit in one of those things all day. I am sure he cannot do much." Mrs. B. Well seems to exemplify lack of insight, condescending manner-isms and focusing in a negative ignorance. Mrs. B. Well may even have the mistaken notion that health is a reward for holiness and vice-versa. "I hope that dear, young man has someone to take care of him," said Mrs. Kindheart. "Maybe he lives in one of those homes that they have for those kinds of people," she continued softly. Mrs. Kindheart may hold precon-ceived notions about what our pilgrim cannot do. "I will bake him a pie," clucked Mrs. Keepemfat. "That poor boy probably has no friends or family. It is too bad that he is so young. He could have really made something out of himself." Well, Mrs. Keepemfat apparently has put her limitations on his hopes, dreams and aspirations. She has probably forgotten about the United States President who led the country through a critical period in American history from a wheelchair.

These are all examples of attitudinal barriers. There are more. As we can see, a person with a disability can be of great worth within a society. Attitudinal barriers fit quite well into Teresa's external trials, for they are trials that come from others. The internal trial, the illness or injury, often has become integrated and is the source of interior strength and patience. In this mansion our attorney pilgrim has a well-developed virtue of patience. One day soon he will meet these women from the Pious Ladies Society, dispel their superficial and restricting assumptions, and enlighten them beyond their wildest imaginings.

Of course attitudinal barriers are not only within the minds of our four pious ladies. They are shared by other good men, women, clergy, and religious. These people will remain in the third mansion as long as they hold onto these attitudes. In the third mansion we can see why the residents keep such false assumptions in their minds. Their lives are based on the dictates of their roles rather than on personal principles. Their perspective of reality is made through external standards and practices. Caught up in the "shoulds" or "should nots" of their own role, they project an unauthentic self-image and project on others false assumptions about their roles, especially when the role of the other does not fall within the "normal" scheme of things.

A classic example here is Sister Charity of Kind Thoughts and Sweet Words. She may represent any person in authority. She is in the third mansion and is the vocation sister for her community. A young woman makes an appointment to see her because she is interested in joining the community. She is working on her Master's degree and has maintained a 3.8 grade point average all through her college years. She is mature, prayerful, wholesome and well-qualified. She lives by herself and is active in many extracurricular activities and service organizations. Oh, yes, she uses a walker. The dear sister takes one look at the young lady and only sees the walker. With no questions asked, she quickly, but kindly and firmly, discourages her from considering the religious life. The sister thinks to herself, "Oh, how can that sweet girl possibly work? How can she be productive in our community? She is so unhealthy." Actually, the young lady only gets sick with a cold about once or twice a year. If Teresa, with all her illnesses and her walking cane would visit with Sister Charity for the same reason, she would probably receive the same response. One wonders what Teresa would have said. Poor Sister Charity!

Teresa explains how other people can be a hardship in the sixth mansion. She is concerned about clergy, religious and others who are not secure within themselves. It would be a danger for our pilgrim to consult with these people even if they may be learned or have a reputation for great holiness. Such people may react with doubt, fear, and condemnation. The misunderstanding or non-understanding of these people could be very distressing to our pilgrim in the sixth mansion. The pilgrim desires to share, but experiences an aloneness that can be eased only by God. When confronted with such negative reactions from others, our pilgrim holds firmly to the reality of God as he manifested himself to the pilgrim. If this certainty is lost, the pilgrim may be besieged by taunts of self-doubt and incriminating thoughts. Our pilgrim has learned a long time ago to rely on the mercy of God. This becomes stronger as advancement within the upper mansions continues. Many times the mercy of God is a cool refuge in the heat of the trials caused by others, and in the aftermath sometimes it seems as if some of these trials never existed.

Although our pilgrim in the sixth mansion is open to gossip, ridicule, criticism, strange stares, and other adverse reactions from people, all is offered to Love for love. The pilgrim is truly grateful for being in this mansion. He or she realizes that much has been received here and much must be given. During the sojourn in this mansion, the pilgrim has no need to reflect upon how he or she stands in humility before God. Humility is now like a comfortable old shoe. Because it is so familiar, one hardly realizes one is wearing it. Humility is an unconscious, luminous process ever present in a person's grace-filled center. The individual's interior humility is strong and is lived in his or her littleness before God. The surrendered heart of the pilgrim is permeated with God's consoling love.

Love without limits

We have learned that love means waiting and holding on in fidelity to the loved one despite the storms of temptation that may arise. Within this mansion the motive behind every thought, word and deed is love. Love prompts the answers to questions and solutions to problems. Love uncovers new questions and is attentive to unrecognized problems. Love enriches our understanding and guides our judgment. Love is the essence of our spiritual maturity and our guide in life. It tells us what to do. It liberates us from a multitude of rules, commandments, and regulations. It requires no conditions, reasons, or accounts. In love, there is no desire to receive anything for what we do. We know that the highest expression of love is sacrifice. Love joins contemplation with action. Love is binding and expansive. We are guided by love alone and find love in everything, everywhere. Here, there is a consistency in our love for God and dear ones no matter what happens. God has given himself far beyond what we could ask for, want, think or desire.

The pilgrim knows that the secret things of God can be found through extraordinary mystical experiences. The loving gazes and ordinary mystical events in the sixth mansion also surpass anything that can be put into words, for they cannot be encompassed by them. So, too, the pilgrim gives to God in ways that go beyond what the pilgrim thought was within the realm of possibility. All is received and given with ardor. The strength to endure the hardships and trials comes only from God. The pilgrim knows that his or her own strength could not endure if it stood alone. Divine strength is essential for survival in this mansion. The journey is long. It requires complete emptying of self and dying to everything that is not of God. The journey is difficult. The pilgrim experiences a variety of physical pains, and sometimes it seems as if the body is about to crumble. The psychological pains come through false accusations, hostility, threats, delusions, or abandonment by loved ones. There are difficulties in being alone or with others. In this mansion there may be times of extraordinary experiences in mystical prayer and there will be times of extraordinary pain. Sometimes health, future plans, hopes, dreams and securities go up in smoke. They vanish in thin air as if they were never even present. A pilgrim is faced with uncertainty. Sometimes it is as if our pilgrim is in a desert with trouble as a lone companion.

Yes, in this mansion there are times of extraordinary suffering. When our pilgrims are confronted with suffering, there are two choices that are available. If they are outside the castle or within the lower mansions, the pilgrims may decide to make themselves and others miserable by choosing the negative aspects of suffering. This means they are filled with complaints, discontent, bitterness, resentment and other self-defeating and confining characteristics. All the characteristics of this choice are limiting and point to withdrawal. They result in an ever decreasing perspective of life for the pilgrims and those associated with them.

The second choice, which is the only choice that makes sense anywhere beyond the third mansion, is to choose the positive aspects of suffering. This means our pilgrims sanctify whatever suffering they have for the love of God. Suffering becomes constructive in the sense that the pilgrims slowly learn how to be resigned to God's plan. The pilgrims, united with God, bring forth the good within themselves and within others. All the characteristics of this choice result in an increase in the experience of life. They affect the pilgrims and all who are with them on the spiritual journey.

So the pilgrim has chosen to face these extraordinary sufferings in a positive manner with God's help. The sufferings make our pilgrim feel as if he or she is wandering in a desert. The bare bones of faith experienced in the fourth mansion are now dry, brittle and sun bleached. There are no consolations or delights, and the extraordinary mystical experiences felt as if they happened a thousand years ago. Our pilgrim lives by faith, a bleak faith that stands alone. All that seemed important has been taken away, obliterated, as if it never existed. There is only a void ahead. The desert is filled with roads of stress, suffering and conflicts. The pilgrim experiences a profound transition through the passion and death of Jesus. The desert holds an atmosphere of death. This can be seen most vividly at its poignant reality in the arid terrain below sea level known as Death Valley. The valley is located largely in California's Inyo County. In 1849 thirty pioneers attempted to find a short cut to the California gold fields by going through it. There were eighteen survivors. The valley was named by one of the women who found much comfort in the twenty-third psalm. Verse four was particularly consoling:

> Even though I walk through the valley of the shadow of death,
> I will fear no evil, for you are with me.

This was a phrase that became excruciatingly real. The valley is marked by the stark presence of death. Formidable places such as Furnace Creek, the Devil's Golf Course, Funeral Mountain, Last Chance Range, the Black Mountains, and Coffin Canyon dot the landscape. The desolate ravaging properties of this desert are second only to the Sahara.

The external signs of the desert give reflection to what is taking place within when extraordinary trials mirror back an interior spiritual desert. There is an abyss, a nothingness, an emptiness. A pilgrim is drained from all he or she can give. Yet, the interior desert remains demanding spiritually, psychologically, emotionally, physically and cognitively. Our pilgrim is alone, and remains alone, without any comforts. The spiritual journey seems to be at a standstill, and all is deadly still. The pilgrim is no longer in control. There is a heaviness and a helplessness. Our pilgrim has hit rock bottom.

The interior desert becomes a place of waiting. One's human nature is really put to the test. The pilgrim is slowly, radically, being purged from all that is not of God. There is a confrontation with a naked, sterile faith. There is prayer without appeal, but slowly, ever so slowly, God begins to reveal his will to the pilgrim as he wishes. God meets the pilgrim in his place and in his time. Although there is emptiness all around, faith and prayer have never been deeper or more real. All conventional paths have been removed. The desert is no place for saccharine saints, for they would surely melt away in the heat. The pilgrim's heart feels like it has turned to stone, yet the ability and desire to pray remains. Slowly the contrasts and paradoxes of the interior desert emerge.

We cannot belong totally to God unless we are detached from everything that is not of God. We cannot be filled unless we are completely empty. We cannot find our lives unless we have lost them. We cannot have all unless we have nothing. We cannot be filled with the white, hot heat of God until we have been drained by the darkness of suffering. We cannot truly forgive others unless we have confronted the evil within ourselves. We become enriched through deprivation. We become strong through our weaknesses. We find wisdom through failure. We understand when we do not understand. Our lives become more simple and they become more profound. We are unaware of our genuine, integrated selves until we find ourselves in Christ. There is movement in stillness. Genuine faith grows when all that seems important has been taken away. God responds to prayer for enlightenment by leaving us empty and desolate.

The interior desert is a dear teacher. Shards of her wisdom have been experienced in desolate places on the spiritual journey, but now it is known that she can make or break our pilgrim. The desert is an excellent proving ground that presents challenges in rapid succession. If our pilgrim does not take the initiative to confront these challenges, there will be spiritual dying and perhaps even death. No mediocrity or complacency is tolerated here. It is not for those who are unable to be accountable or responsible for themselves and rigidly and blindly follow traditions, structures, rituals, or customs. It is all or nothing. There is no ordinary routine to fall back on. It is a day to day spiritual survival. The pilgrim confronts the untamed and stands face to face with an incomprehensible God. There are no spiritual roles, nor duties, nor things to do. Our pilgrim stands totally exposed before God. An individual does not babble here. One can only be mute to know God as God.

The interior desert experience is not chosen by our pilgrim. Sometimes it comes unexpectedly like a bolt out of the blue which strikes and leaves one with a total dependency on God. No one knows how long it will last or how many desert experiences there will be in a lifetime. A person realizes more deeply and more intensely God's sovereignty over all. The desert is the place where God chooses to reveal himself and lets the pilgrim see things as they are from his vision. It is a time when God scrapes away at the pilgrim with his file until the pilgrim becomes shredded, and his or her dreams evaporate into a vapor. It is a space where blistering hot winds scorch the desert dry depths within the heart. Hope is saturated with the sands of fear. Sharing and caring have become desolate in their drudgery. The pilgrim is worn in weakness. The desert is also a place, time and space where our pilgrim becomes espoused in true faith and God speaks in the secret places of the heart. The words of Hosea ring loud and clear through the dry yet pungent air: "So I will allure her. I will lead her into the desert and speak to her heart" (2:16).

The interior desert experience comes to a close with spiritual realities that are neither measurable nor expressible, yet they are revealed through an intense, new vision of life. We have learned that all things work together for God's good. The soft rains have quenched the parched dryness within. We are distinctly refreshed and revitalized. Despite this tremendous experience, we feel no need to be different, unique, or set apart from the human family. We quietly bring the interior desert to humanity and gently release it where it is needed. We bring the peace of Christ to a battered world. We represent hope to the hopeless and compassion to the hateful, harsh and hurting. We represent life in death, beauty in ugliness, serenity in turmoil, unity in difficulty and diversity, and an interior wholeness and holiness amid external fragmentation and destruction.

Yes, the interior desert may come without warning like a flash of lightning, or a sudden earthquake. There seems to be no reason why it began but, on occasion, the desert experience can be initiated by a very real occurrence. These life experiences usually cause a pause, or a complete stop, along a life's journey. Life seems suspended for a time until the trauma has been worked through. Some traumatic life experiences that may trigger an interior desert are: termination from work, a failure, disillusionment, or exhaustion after putting years of time, effort and dedication into a job, sudden and prolonged mental problems, diagnosis of a terminal or incurable disease. The sudden death of a loved one, a move to another state, climate, or country, a long stay, flat on one's back, in a hospital, a terrifying event, or any other traumatic experience may be a factor in leading to an interior desert. Whatever the cause, we cannot doubt that the desert experience holds the searing breath or the forceful wind of God's Spirit. The desert can be a rich place. It is time set apart from the mainstream of the spiritual life. If we are very quiet in the interior desert, we may feel God gently pulling us back together. Like Humpty Dumpty after the fall, God can do what all the king's horses and all the king's men could not do. God puts the fragmented pieces of our broken and shattered lives back together again, and we are left feeling better than ever before.

A key sign of growth in the sixth mansion is the ability to recognize God in whatever form he desires to manifest himself. God's beauty and grandeur, shown through the extraordinary mystical experiences, confront the pilgrims with themselves and pinpoint all their small internal deficiencies. If the pilgrims are able to discern this, the mystical experiences have been placed in their proper perspective. A danger here is that the pilgrims may become lost in the mystical realm of God and think themselves as seraphim or cherubim or any other number of the nine choirs of heavenly spirits who praise God all day. To avoid this notion Teresa urges that time should be spent meditating on the humanity of Jesus. Our pilgrims do not become angelic beings through the effects of these extraordinary mystical experiences. They still remain in their mortal bodies. They still must eat and sleep. If our pilgrims feel they should be granted the privilege of being in an angelic state and act the part, they will only do harm to themselves and drive other people around them crazy. In order to prevent a state of artificial mysticism, the pilgrims should keep their eyes, hearts, and minds on Jesus in all his humanness. Teresa suggested that the pilgrims would resemble imbeciles if they sat around and waited for more extraordinary mystical experiences to keep them in their mystical stupor. This stupor is not only a miserable state from the spiritual standpoint, it is quite contrary to mental stability. God gives as he chooses so, pilgrims, get to work as Jesus did, and do not mope around waiting for something that may not even happen. Mary, the perfect contemplative and the recipient of the highest graced gift from God, had one vision. After that, she did not spend her time in mystical pursuits. She, very humbly and very simply, visited her cousin. Then, after her Son was born, she washed the dishes, swept the floor, and did other ordinary things a loving wife and mother does.

As our pilgrims reach the end of their journey in the sixth mansion, they find that everything within their lives serves God's purpose. God is very close. He is experienced as a purifying, transforming fire. The lights and wisdom on this journey cause a genuine transformation in a person's actions. There is a sincere and deeper imitation of Jesus' life which is evident to others who interact with our pilgrims. God has spoken to the inmost heart. The pilgrims have grown in courage and fortitude. These virtues are very necessary for this time of betrothal. There is pain mixed with tranquility. The pilgrims are aware of God's absence and his presence. Now is the time when our pilgrims leave the path of the spiritual journey to fly in abandonment to God.

The many aspects of purification

Within the sixth mansion purification becomes a way of life. It is a washing that continues day by day and matures one through stark self-evaluation.

Purification, the cleansing of the masked self from the authentic self is possible when others are present in a pilgrim's living and working environments. Cleansing comes through learning to live and work with others more effectively. Living with others keeps an individual in touch with his or her own idiosyncrasies. There is a deeper realization of one's quirks, shortcomings and deficits. Sometimes it is amazing how other people respond to them! If they are hurtful to others, the pilgrim knows that some revisions must be made. Being continually reminded of one's warts through stringent self-evaluation or through the observations of others keeps one's feet firmly on the ground. The reaction of others to a person's negative traits knocks down any notion or false illusion that he or she is very special in the sight of God no matter how many extraordinary mystical experiences one has had. Being in close contact with others is a constant reminder of an individual's brokenness, humanness, woundedness, and frailty. Purification is gently at work when a pilgrim does not let these areas interfere with his or her routine or daily interactions with others.

Purification continues through our pilgrim's own views, thoughts or opinions about the people with whom he or she lives, works, or meets during any occasion. Throughout life a person interacts with a wide variety of people. Each person has a separate and unique personality filled with an assortment of traits. Along the road of life our pilgrim may meet those who are shy, and those who know no strangers. There are some who hold grudges and others who forgive easily. There are the insecure, those who have it all together, the rationalizers and the romantics. Those who always blame contrast those who always apologize. There are task-oriented people, whose work becomes their life, and care-giving people who are motivated by love. One may meet those who intellectualize, those who scapegoat, eloquent talkers and dynamic doers. Some are dour and others have a flair for the dramatic. There are people who know nothing and those who know it all. People who are deadly serious balance the sweetly sentimental. People who are angry and frustrated oppose the joyful and liberated. People who pride themselves because they are very self-controlled counteract emotional people who fly into a tizzy at a minor incident. There are the nitpicker, the braggers, the merrymakers, and the jokesters. The orderly balance with the disorderly. The headstrong are contrary to the pushover. There are those who are dependable and those who cannot accept responsibility. There are the lovers, the haters, and those who are indifferent or ambivalent. There are people who are suspicious or trusting, crude or courteous, distinguished or playful. There are the conformers, the reformers, and the informers. There are those who are kind, sensitive, ebullient and affirming. Then there are those who are rigid, obtuse, moody and disarming. This list is endless, but it will stop here. The purpose in presenting the variants within personality traits is to illustrate how different people can serve as a cleansing agent in the sixth mansion. The gentle reader may even have felt some negative reactions when he or she was reading this list.

It goes without saying that there are people who will rub one the wrong way. When an individual is rubbing elbows with people whose tendencies have an abrasive nature day after day, week after week, and year after year, the individual has the opportunity to use these abrasives as a mode for purification. A pilgrim shows sound signs of genuine holiness when he or she is able to get along with and work together well with others who are not compatible with the pilgrim's nature. The pilgrim, in learning to live and work with others, has cleansed himself or herself from vague judgments, undue criticism and irrelevant statements directed to or said about the person with incongruous traits. Growth in the sixth mansion is made when there is the ability to be amiable, natural, and sensitive to those whose personality traits are annoying, irritating, exasperating or down right nauseating.

An observable sign of this growth is indicated by decreased use of such phrases as: "He bugs me," "She gets on my nerves," "That individual gives me the creeps," "He drives me up the wall," or "I cannot stand her." These external verbalizations are replaced by an internal groan or moan (for even in the sixth mansion one remains delightfully human). After that internal recognition of dissatisfaction has been acknowledged, our pilgrim makes an effort to rise above the situation. It may be of help to focus on a soothing, calming trait this individual has, thus neutralizing the grinding quality of the irritating trait. It may be of help to eliminate thoughts that focus on how the vexing traits of others affect one. These thoughts are as useful as a damp squib. As time passes and growth continues, a person learns to replace negative thoughts with positive musings about the goodness and loveableness of those who irritate.

When a pilgrim finds that it is easy to get along with a great number of people most of the time, a significant gain in purifying self from self has been made. The irritants that bothered our pilgrim before are now only small pinpricks that are immaterial. The pinpricks will continue throughout life, but they are not even worth talk or thought. An exception here is when an abrasive trait is significantly exasperating to a number of people. Then the person with the abrasive trait must be confronted in a therapeutic manner.

In dealing with difficult relationships in the sixth mansion, the pilgrim learns to be tolerant with self and with others. There is a great self-discipline shown in an individual's words and actions. One thinks before one speaks to avoid undue harsh words. A person overlooks a great deal. One is able to let tension, slights, and related negatives flow off one as water flows off the back of a duck. The pilgrim becomes lenient toward others and easily forgives them. There is an introspection to see why the pinpricks irritate, and perhaps laughter, because the reasons behind them were so insignificant. The pilgrim finds laughter at his or her own personal quirks. The pilgrim knows that all is in God's hands, and in the light of eternity, many things are not nearly as serious as one thinks them to be. This is also reflected on the pilgrim's self. The self is not taken as seriously as before, nor is it viewed as being so very important. There is a gentleness and a patience with one's being that was unknown before. A merriment permeates the pilgrim and blossoms into laughter at the serendipity within the ordinary events of life. Every person has a few strange qualities. Many times a person is more loveable because of his or her quirks. Our pilgrim will find that his or her frustration level will decrease as he or she makes progress through the sixth mansion. The pilgrim becomes relaxed and nothing much upsets him or her. Through an easygoing attitude our pilgrim finds a loveableness toward the bit of strange bird that exists in other people and which also exists in the pilgrim. God works through people in many ways!

Throughout life a person is involved in a multitude of group activities. Being a member of a group is an integral part of a person's life. This begins at birth when an individual is born into a family group and continues on through play groups, learning groups, interest groups, recreational groups, groups at work, and groups at prayer. At all stages of life a person can belong to one or many groups. The quality of a person's interactions within a group is dependent on how effectively that person functions in a group situation.

The following question may present itself: Why is group dynamics being proposed in the sixth mansion? Teresa notes that the closer pilgrims come to God the more effectively they will be able to relate to others. A mature spirituality is congruent with a maturity in social relationships. Because the sixth mansion represents a high level of holiness, the pilgrims in it should be highly skilled in relating to different types of people. Those who are spiritually mature give expression of this maturity through other areas within their lives that are equally mature. It is impossible to be in this mansion and possess the emotional development of a pubescent. It is impossible to be in this mansion and possess interpersonal relationships that are characteristic of the adolescent.

Because this is not an in-depth discussion of the stages of development within groups, the group presented will be rather unique. For the sake of simplicity our pilgrim finds himself or herself in a group that is composed of pilgrims from the higher mansions. This can be a community group, a family group, a work group, or any group in which all members possess a high level of spiritual maturity. The group may be composed of all men, or all women, or for optimal balancing and complementary integration, both men and women. When this group comes together to discuss a topic, several factors can be assumed. Each person is able to observe and listen carefully because the art of sincerely loving and caring for others has been learned in the previous mansions. The members of this group are interpersonally competent. The group climate is one that maintains a high level of trust, openness and communication. The members are able to work together in a cooperative way. There is a supportive and affirmative bearing for each group member. Each member recognizes his or her own special pettinesses, set ways, defense mechanisms, emotional blocks and sensitive areas and tries to override them when they interfere with smooth group interaction. Each member holds a high respect for the integrity of other group members and the unique workings of God in each person's life. Each person values the contributions of other members, even though there may not be an agreement with them. The good of the group is placed ahead of any member's own particular opinions, views or interests. Each person is able to see past his or her own perspective and benefits from the input, both verbal and nonverbal, of others. Each person seeks the working of God in each group member regarding the task at hand and seeks the working of God within the group as a collective, corporate unit working toward a common good. If there is any personal dissatisfaction, discontent or frustrations when decisions have been reached, they are verbalized and discussed before the group terminates. If there are intense personal feelings or emotions that have been aroused during the group meeting, they can be burned out by a fast game of racquetball or other similar appropriate activity that involves sweat and physical exertion after the group closes. Because of the degree of spiritual maturity within the group, each member recognizes the futility of emotional outbursts, heated arguments, or knock down, drag out fist fights during a group meeting.

When our pilgrim finds himself or herself contributing to a group discussion, there are many positions he or she may take. Because a person is in the sixth mansion, he or she has the ability to contribute from several positions within a group during a specific group meeting. A brief description of these positions will be presented so that our pilgrim may reflect on his or her own strong areas, weak areas, and ability to change positions and contribute from them.

The person who suggests new ideas is appropriately called the initiator. The information seeker asks for clarification of facts, figures, ideas and other data related to the task. The information giver contributes facts, figures and other necessary data. The opinion seeker requests clarification of opinions, values or beliefs. The elaborator spells out suggestions and is concerned about necessary details regarding the development of the items under discussion. The coordinator clarifies relationships and keeps things running along a smooth course. The originator defines the position of the group with respect to its goals. The evaluator critiques and compares the accomplishments of the group to some set standard. The energizer prods the group into action and keeps things moving. The procedural technician expedites group movement by performing routine tasks. The encourager praises, agrees with, supports and accepts the contributions of others. The harmonizer mediates differences between members. The compromiser changes his or her own behavior to maintain group harmony. The gate keeper facilitates and regulates communication. The standard setter expresses standards for the group to achieve. The observer takes notes and interprets and presents information about group process. The follower goes along with the movement of the group. The comedian releases the tensions and seriousness within a group through wit and whimsy. Each of these positions facilitates growth in group dynamics.

Within a pilgrim's interpersonal relationship with a loved friend, there has been an elimination of personal defenses and a destruction of walls that may keep an individual safe and secure. It is a time of continual unmasking. A great sense of painful nakedness is present during this process. There is a deep trusting in the other, but because a person is very vulnerable, there is also the fear of being betrayed and hurt and a feeling of being unprotected. One's character is totally exposed and one freely shares personal information that comes from the depths of one's heart. A human being's empty spaces and weak places are known by the other. In spite of the fears, there is a deep sensing that each is within the other, that two are as one rooted together by love. At the depth of their beings a union remains solid despite painful surface encounters. This type of relationship is not easy. There is much personal involvement. The two people involved have risked a deep love for each other and have found a deep anguish, but through the pain of love they have learned how to transcend themselves. Transcendence is the fairest flower of intimacy. It teaches them to hold on in trust when all outside is dark. They believe in each other when there are no reasons to believe. Love continues to burn even when surface pain seems to extinguish its light and heat. To really know the demands of intimacy requires a continual self-disclosure. When there is self-disclosure there are no masks, no games, no retreats to an inner safety. Through self-disclosure each holds the other with a precious reverence and respect. The remembrance of these deeply shared moments become sustaining forces in times of trouble or weary routine. They give an uplifting dimension to a pilgrim's daily occupations and routine contacts.

The sixth mansion requires an extraordinary faith, trust, and confidence in God. Evidence of these traits in our pilgrim is reflected by the extraordinary faith, trust and confidence he or she has in the loved other. Because these traits are now so profound, they act as a catalyst to strengthen the sincerity of one's faith, trust and confidence shown to others who cross one's path from day to day.

The sixth mansion is a time when there is a gradual filling up of spiritual knowledge and wisdom that comes from one's still point. This knowledge and wisdom come from a deep experience in the sharing of the passion, death and resurrection of Jesus. It is a true gut level journey with Jesus. The pilgrim becomes concealed with Christ in God. Because one has been wounded with an intense love for Jesus, there is a great desire to be alone with him after one's duties of the day are completed. Any unexpected free time is spent in solitude. The solitude is comparable to the periodic times when Jesus went to the desert to pray to his Father. Solitude is a time of loving intimacy. Jesus is the pilgrim's continual and direct bonding with and to the Father. Jesus is the source of all that is good and loving and obedient and forgiving. Jesus has dared the pilgrim to touch him. The pilgrim now shares in his pain, is bound in his wounds, and responds to the contempt shown him by love. A person is living Jesus by sharing in his passion and responding as he did by reflecting God's love. One is living Jesus by sharing in his resurrection and responding as he did by radiating the greatness of God's love to all.

The following prayer poem will mark a close to our pilgrim's journey through the sixth mansion. Its beauty speaks to the heart. This poem comes from the Poor Clare Monastery in Aptos, California. It was given to the sisters there. The author, as far as we know, is unknown.

Now you are with me,
Lord of all Mercy,
Always so patient,
Setting aright;
Help me be empty,
Open, receptive,
Always accepting
Lord of all Light.

Then I can follow
Where you are leading,
Walk the unceasing
Way of the Cross;
With you before me,
Suffering Servant,
Even in torment,
There is no loss.

Only the awesome,
Mystery-hidden,
Silent, redemptive,
Secret of pain;
In its self-giving,
Full immolation,
Love is the secret,
Love is the gain.

Keep me, my Savior,
Little and humble,
Gratefully prostrate
Here at your feet;
Your mind is my mind,
Your love enfolds me,
Nothing else matters,
I am complete.

Seventh Mansion

THE MYSTICAL MARRIAGE

Our seventh mansion is the mansion of the mystical marriage. The tiny seed planted in the second mansion is now an exquisite flower in full bloom. The pilgrim visualizes Jesus as he really is through a transforming union. The prayer of union is complete in all its intensity. Communication is only possible now through a deep silence.

It seems as if so much has been said about the spiritual journey that there is little left to tell. Not so, Teresa counsels, for God's greatness and his works are boundless. It is impossible to write of all the mysteries of God. They are infinite. They are without limits.

Yet when one reaches the seventh mansion one is struck dumb. It is so awesome that our pilgrim becomes covered with confusion when he or she tries to describe it. It seems as if words are meaningless. Descriptions, analogies and symbols fall apart. This land of transforming union is beyond the reach of words. A person can only make awkward attempts at describing what has happened here, and this is what will follow.

One's bumbling efforts make sense only when they are converted into an ongoing song that sings of God's blessings. The seventh mansion is filled with the celestial light of heaven. The melody from the song of blessings rings joyfully through this resplendent light and echoes from every corner of this most interior chamber.

The good God calls the pilgrim to this mansion. When our pilgrim steps over the threshold, he or she becomes united to the triune God. There is a complete and total transformation in God. An individual is engulfed in his magnificent, fiery splendor. This will never be repeated. Within the engulfment the three persons of the Trinity are distinct yet remain as one in substance and purpose. At this point the pilgrim can do nothing or say nothing. One knows one is in the seventh mansion because it is like an individual is in heaven. His or her spirit is made one with God. Intimacy with God takes place at the innermost center of a pilgrim's being which is inaccessible to all save God. It is as if two lighted flames have joined forever into one. The pilgrim feels like a raindrop that has fallen into a river, or a stream that has entered the sea. The self is finally dead to self. The long journey is ended. The center mansion has been reached. The pilgrim lives now in God. There are no desires for spiritual consolations, spiritual delights, or extraordinary mystical experiences. There are no desires for hardships, trials, or suffering. There is a holy indifference to everything. An interior freedom enables the pilgrim to give himself or herself unreservedly to the service of God. Holiness is found in whatever happens, and life is lived with a cheerful abandonment. The pilgrim no longer lives as himself or herself, but lives fully from Jesus dwelling within. As each day passes the pilgrim becomes more amazed at the divine Trinitarian truths that are revealed from his or her deep still center.

Teresa experienced the mystical marriage through an intellectual vision of Jesus. This can happen to our pilgrim in the same way, but Teresa states that there are many other ways in which one enters the seventh mansion. Whatever the way, there is a distinct difference between residing in the sixth mansion and residing in the seventh mansion. A union with Jesus in the seventh mansion is indissoluble and indelible. It is similar to Jesus' union with his Father when he was on earth. There is no restlessness or loneliness here because God seems absent. Now he is present within, forever.

In this mansion the pilgrim's heart is almost always in a state of quietness. There are no worries about the wiles of the evil one. All is calm. A safe security surrounds our pilgrim. Security at last! Security supports and sustains our pilgrim as long as he or she resides in the heart of God. A separation from this heart could cause a fall. Our pilgrim has not lost the capacity to make a decision that goes against love. Even though our pilgrim has reached the seventh mansion, there still will be days of doubt, depression and discouragement. There will also be temptations. Usually, solid reasons are behind these feelings, but a person will not be overcome by them unless he or she chooses to be. Desires that go against love will come, but they should be defeated because of an individual's deep stability in God.

The seventh mansion is not a perpetual dwelling on cloud nine. It is not a state of perfect and total fulfillment. It is not an eternal nirvana, nor is it a merging with the cosmic consciousness. These terms only profane the seventh mansion.

There is no continual feeling of absolute bliss inside the seventh mansion. Growth still takes place here. Teresa vehemently states that if we cease to go forward, we can only go backward. We do not experience a feeling of "this is it," or an exultant musing of having "made it." We do not put down the armor of battle. Although we are very close, the promised land has not been reached. If we cease to forge ahead anywhere along the spiritual journey, we may fall backwards into a swamp that is full of mold, mildew and decay. Yes, this can happen even within the seventh mansion, for the pure love that the human being radiates during the mystical marriage is not the perfect love that is the essence of the beatific vision. We hope to experience this perfect love after we have died. However, as long as we live on this earth we still maintain the capacity to turn away from God.

There are no frequent fiery feelings of great devotion in the seventh mansion. After a pilgrim crosses the threshold, the deep fiery intensity of God's love is still felt, but it is subdued. It is now an ever present glow experienced as perpetual warmth that comes from white hot coals. If God's love continued in the intensity that was felt during the marriage encounter at the entrance of the seventh mansion, our pilgrim could not go about his or her daily routine or stand to be alone or with others. Now the pilgrim's love for God is ever present, and ever constant, and flows from the heart. This is also expressed in the same manner in God's love for the pilgrim. Heart is in heart. Spirit is in spirit. His love is as quiet as snowflakes, gently and silently falling on a field of snow on a still winter's night. The workings of God within are noiseless. He and the heart of one's spirit rejoice together in the deepest silence possible. All activities of the mind are subdued and still. Deepest depths have joined in silent music with deepest depths. The pilgrim's every breath is a tacit expression of God's love. A person finds a tremendous joy in time spent in solitude with the indwelling Three. The trials and sufferings of life do not disturb, nor do they take away the deep and abiding peace of the seventh mansion. One is not concerned about the past or the future.

Jesus is now the life of the pilgrim. There is a profound understanding of this. Through him our pilgrim becomes one with the Father. There is an interest and total concern for him and with him. A triune unity of love, bound by the Spirit, saturates the pilgrim. To know this love, which surpasses all knowledge, is to be filled with the fullness of God. The pilgrim finds a permanent abiding and a lasting repose in triune love. Love places all cares at the feet of Jesus, and the pilgrim finds peace in knowing that these cares are truly the concerns of the triune God. As the Father was the life of Jesus when he was on earth, and the source of his power and wisdom and love, so now is Jesus the life of the pilgrim. There is continual enjoyment of the divine companionship. The pilgrim strives to be the total goodness of Jesus. The pilgrim strives to be for others as Jesus was. The pilgrim now changes from seeing God in all things, to seeing all things in God.

Union with the triune God does not mean that our pilgrim becomes so absorbed in what has happened that all else is forgotten. It is quite the contrary. There is much more occupation with tasks that pertain to the service of God. During these duties and after they are completed, the pilgrim remains in the enjoyable company of the divine Three. There is a great contentment that emanates from the continuous triune presence within. Because of this presence, the pilgrim goes about with an even greater caution than before. Our pilgrim desires not to displease God in anything. The pilgrim knows well that he or she could easily depart from the path of love, but even to think about a thought that would cause a departure causes our pilgrim to tremble.

Within the seventh mansion the pilgrim becomes one with the people of God. There is a deep concern, a Christ concern, for all the pilgrims who are journeying inside the castle and for all those outside of the castle. The pilgrim sees more than ever the pathetic state of those people outside the walls of the castle and remembers well the atrocious environment of the first mansion. It is the pilgrim's loving obligation and sacred trust to sincerely pray for those forlorn souls in hopes that they will see the light.

The heart of the pilgrim in the seventh mansion is totally selfless. It is filled with the desire to pray to God and do works of service for others. Neither prayer nor work ever get out of balance. One could not exist without the other. Prayer and work are poised in delicate harmony and give life only when they are joined together in equal proportions within the pilgrim's life. A pilgrim's prayerful presence permeates the other areas of his or her life with a boundless joy. Prayer gives one the strength to serve others, and this service gives concerned action to prayer.

The works a person does need not be grand. All that is required from the prayer flow is to do the task at hand with love. God does not look at the greatness of the work. Small tasks have the same value in the eyes of God as great tasks, if each is done with love. A pilgrim's deep life of prayer gives him or her the readiness to want always to assist others. To become as Jesus in the seventh mansion is to experience the depths of his prayer and the depths of his goodness toward others. All flow from the profundity of his compassionate love.

True compassion becomes authentically integrated when our pilgrim lovingly, graciously and totally submits to the will of God in his or her own life and in the lives of others. The greater one is permeated with compassion, the greater the tendency will be not to question God regarding the "whys" of providence. An individual understands this if he or she does not offer God advice about what to do with people who no longer seem to be productive and successful members of society or the Church.

How do we view people who are set aside from the mainstream of life? What is our honest reaction to the young adult who has been in a coma for the past five years? How about the Vietnam war veteran who has no functional use of his arms or legs; or the ten-year-old child who because he is severely developmentally delayed cannot walk or talk or feed, dress, groom or clean himself? What is our immediate reaction to the listless faces of the elderly who line the halls of a county-operated convalescent hospital and have no desire to live, or a dear relative who is going through the last agonies of a cancer she has been battling for years? How do we respond to a woman in her late twenties who must be fed through a feeding tube that is inserted in her stomach, or the high school student body president who was tragically burned and maimed in a car accident? How about the forty-five-year-old man who is unable to overtly express the difference between a shoe and a spoon?

In the lower mansions we often hear the phrase, "Why does God permit such things?" or, "Why doesn't the good Lord take him or her?" It is only human to use these phrases on a few occasions. However, in the higher mansions we seek to look at a situation with the eyes of God. Answers to the questions regarding things that leave us unsettled many times cannot be given for they are beyond human understanding. We have learned to be patient toward the unresolved. We have learned to quickly forget our own ideas on the value of the lives lived by these people. To look with the eyes of God is to see their pain and their suffering in whatever form it takes and see it as an extension of Christ's suffering. God uses the weak to confuse the strong. Within the heart of God anyone who suffers can be a channel of God's life and love that heals the hurting world. It is God who gives life and sustains it. He knows when each person will come home to him. The length of time and the degree in which a person suffers is all a part of God's mysterious plan. To see it as his plan, when his plan is embraced in love and surrender, is to bring out the grace in the suffering. The suffering, then, becomes redemptive and it is transformed into a beautiful manifestation of true compassion.

Teresa shows us how true compassion flows from the heart when it is born from redemptive suffering. The pain that causes the suffering is acknowledged but not emphasized. Although it is very real, the extent of the pain is usually known only to God, the person experiencing it, and significant others who are trained to assist the person in living with it. Redemptive suffering is normally expressed without fanfare. It is a quiet, knowing manifestation of true compassion. There is nothing overt about it. All is given to God in silence. Great activities that require enormous physical strength and momentous achievements that require boundless energy, even though they are a part of the work of God, do not fit into redemptive suffering. Redemptive suffering is experienced when one understands how God reveals himself to each person to the extent that the person accepts his or her own smallness, weakness, littleness, and wound-edness. Jesus showed the limitlessness of God's love through his poverty, abandonment, suffering and death. Through these he showed his great compassion.

Redemptive suffering springs from the heart of Jesus. Bernard of Clairvaux once said, "The most intimate dialogue between man and God was that of suffering in the embrace possible only on the cross." It was then that Jesus released into the world the power of his resurrection. At the hour of his greatest suffering Jesus showed to all his greatest compassion. He gave us Mary as our mother. He forgave all unconditionally even his cruelest enemies. He totally surrendered himself to his Father. Redemptive suffering through an individual complements the redemptive work of Christ. The pain within our lives makes us realize how little control we have over our own lives, and how dependent we are on the mercy of God. Jesus makes our pain bearable and transforms it through his love. When our pain is transformed, it can be used for the sake of dear ones and others who may need it. In the context of redemptive suffering, pain can purify, refine and strengthen prayer. Here pain can be developed into a creative potential and carried in a joy that reflects the glory of Easter. Redemptive suffering opens us up to a greater sensitivity to God, a deeper awareness of ourselves, and a deeper awareness of the fragility and neediness within others. Through redemptive suffering Jesus shares his life with us and we share our lives with him. God and humankind truly come together in the unity and mystery of the redemption.

Teresa embodied redemptive suffering in more ways than one. She carried it with her through daily pain. She also expressed it through a solicitous love and concern for her struggling pilgrims. Living the mystery of redemptive suffering is not limited to those who share in the passion of Christ through some form of pain. It is also expressed through compassionate care-giving people who share the vulnerability, the fear, the brokenness and the bewilderment of those who carry a specific pain. As a compassionate care giver becomes more intimate with God through prayer, he or she becomes more responsible to others and develops a greater capacity to understand, love and accept them. This capacity is not directed to the specific pain of the other. It is directed toward the individual as a unique person who happens to have a specific pain. There is a caring for the human being, rather than for the patient or the client. The compassionate care giver is transpierced by the pain of the other, and in this way the redemptive quality of the pain is shared by him or her. Through this unique sharing both people participate in and are the recipient of the ongoing drama of the redemption.

Dyadic forms of redemptive suffering can be manifested in many ways. It may be expressed steadfastly and profoundly through a long-term caring that continues for many, many years. This team effort is grounded in deep trust and confidence. The care giver and the wounded person work as a unit to confront the challenges of a chronic and debilitating disease. A journey down this road may be filled with frustrations and difficulties, but the wounded one does not lose heart. There is a great comfort and strength in knowing that one is traveling along this path with a genuine care giver who sincerely understands. Oftentimes a gentle handshake from a care giver of this caliber speaks more loudly than the kindest words or the most sophisticated of medical techniques. It does so because this caring touch is personalizing, supportive, calming and reassuring.

Dyadic redemptive suffering is expressed by the college student who visits her "adopted grandmother" in a retirement home week after week. It may be seen through the foster grandpa who continually visits his deaf and blind teenage "granddaughter" at a state residential care hospital. She was left at the doorstep of this hospital a few months after she was born by her parents who have not been seen since. It may be seen in all its simplicity by the quiet extension of a hand to hold when an individual is walking over a rough patch of ground. Within a dyadic form of redemptive suffering the pain and weakness of both people serve as a potential for growth and are a cause for praise and thanks to God. Their shared weaknesses and strengths have become channels for a mutual give and take, and a greater understanding of what it means to be authentically human.

Teresa's prayer was refined through her redemptive suffering. It was through her suffering that she became increasingly conscious of the suffering Christ. His suffering became her own. Teresa was a woman of compassion and total surrender. Her prayer was compassionate as were her actions. She shows us that by being honest with our weaknesses and pains (and everyone has them), and cheerfully accepting them, we become more aware of and vulnerable to the needs of the world and its pain. Compassionate prayer develops when we hold the suffering world in our hearts during prayer.

Our prayer can only become compassionate when we are truly aware of the wounded people and the wounded places on the earth. For most of us this awareness comes through the various elements of the news media. If we have no connection with news from the outside world, it is hardly possible that our prayer can be rooted in the broken places and the broken people that currently inhabit the earth. Several contemplative communities of religious have integrated a short segment of time for world news into their day. By watching the news the incentive to wholeheartedly pray, let us say, for the end of a war in progress is intensified through the manifold destructive effects of the war which are actually seen and heard on the TV news. However, time spent watching the news should be reduced if signs of desensitization to its violence becomes apparent.

Compassionate prayer offers and holds people, especially those who do not know him, in God's providence. It is a prayer of hope for wounded people, said that they may change through a greater openness and receptivity to him. Compassionate prayer requires a heart depth union with those for whom one prays. There is a sincere concern for them and a very real sharing of their pain. Pain can take on many forms: the unrelenting hunger pains of the starving child, the frustrating pain of the overworked health care professional, the indecisiveness of the insecure student, the loneliness of the bag lady or the street bum, the helplessness of the young mother, alone, with five children to raise. These many hurts become the life force which keeps prayer flowing through the heart. These prayers are not said in order to change God's actions within these people. They are to be a means of union between God and the people, and a way in which the people find God touching them through the incidents of their lives. The one who prays holds the people in prayer very profoundly and holds them in God very tenderly.

Prayer cannot be called sincere compassionate prayer if there is not a compassionate action that flows from it. Compassionate prayer without compassionate action stalemates into an artificial pious act, a romantic spiritual sentiment, or a detached sanctimonious indifference. Compassionate prayer with compassionate action extends the Christ of compassion to others through the caring of prayer. When praying for large groups far away that suffer from persecution, the ravages of war, hunger, poverty or other oppressions, a follow-up action may be made through the various modes of the news media. For people who ask for prayers or for whom prayers are promised, a phone call, a letter of concern inquiring how one is getting along, or a note of remembrance are examples of compassionate action that flows from compassionate prayer. Any mode of follow through shows sincere concern, love and care and can be an assurance to the receiver that he or she is still being held in prayer and not forgotten.

Let us look at an example here. A sincere young Christian has just requested prayers from a member of the local contemplative monastery. He is stepping out into adult life and wants to manifest his faith in some way. This young man would feel much more love and support if the person who is praying for him takes a sincere interest in what he is doing in order to find ways to express his faith. Perhaps some helpful suggestions would be in order, or when the young man is visiting the monastery the prayer person may just be there to listen and hold a frightened and insecure hand. To pray for others, yet show no overt concern for what is happening in their lives, is a cold prayer indeed. We are reminded here of a story about a minister (or any other person engaged in the visitation apostolate). A minister made a visit to a young mother in his parish. The mother had a twelve-year-old son who was physically disabled. Her husband had deserted her two years ago, and the son was completely dependent on his mother for all his daily needs. She had to bathe him, dress him, feed him, toilet him, and transfer him whenever he had to be moved to or from his wheelchair. The minister's visit was the first one he had with this young mother. It was very short. He gravely commented on how well the mother was carrying her large, heavy cross in life. He promised to pray for her, gave her his blessing and left. There was no mention of a return visit.

This is a vivid example of how prayer can be rather cool. The minister would have done much better if the promised prayer was followed up with a return visit. During the time before the visit, the minister could get a list of qualified baby-sitters in the parish who would be willing to stay with the boy so his mother might have some time for herself, or he could obtain a list of service organizations within the community that may be of assistance to the mother. If this information is not readily available, he could direct her to an individual or agency that offers professional services in her area of need. Another option would be for the minister to sincerely listen during his next visit. Here is where compassion is expressed in a "being" rather than in some specific action.

Many people know that in times of suffering and pain, words can be awkward. This is so often seen at funerals or at intensive care units in hospitals. The simple presence of someone who cares is more comforting than most words. The caring expresses itself through a gentle hug, a hand to hold, or a shoulder to cry on. A sharing of the pain can come through a reassuring touch, a smile, and maybe even a laugh. Genuine concern is not filled with flowery phrases, pious platitudes, or techniques to change the present behavior of the broken person. Rather it is being with, and acceptance of, that person as he or she is within that moment in time. An individual's unobtrusive, unpretentious presence may give a greater healing because the wounded one is free to be vulnerable, fragile and out of control in the presence of the caring person. The caring person then symbolizes resurrection and hope. It is helpful to remember that there is a deep purification that comes with the uninhibited shedding of tears. This cleansing may initiate healing.

Compassionate prayer bonded with compassionate action represents a caring that is total, unconditional and without reservations. It also represents a sound and loving connection of the infinity of the infinite God with the frailty of the finite human. Compassionate prayer cannot stand alone. Compassionate action must flow from it in order for this prayer to be valid. Conversely, neither can compassionate action stand alone. Compassionate action without prayer is void of a life-giving force that is rooted in God. It is void of the gospel dimension that unites it with the loving work of Jesus. In order for compassionate action to be valid, it must radiate from a heart that is centered in prayer.

What are the elements that make a good work a compassionate action? Often there are subtle characteristics behind the good work that are not related to compassion. We may desire to control those we work with by manipulation. We may desire to control the time spent working with the oppressed so that when we are tired or fed up we can return to a comfortable middle class existence. We may feel noble or gallant because we have sacrificed our time and energies. We may use pitying, condescending, patronizing, or demeaning thoughts, words and actions when working with others. We may do good works in order to relieve our own guilt. We may have a need to be liked, praised, recognized or accepted. We may see those with whom we work as poor unfortunate objects to be pitied or stereotyped together in a project to which we are dedicated. We may want to be busy to avoid pain or loneliness or problems. There may be a concern for others, but the concern is motivated by an underlying hostility. We may pride ourselves in our own goodwill. We may be caught up in the tendrils of do-goodism that may feed an oblivious optimism and cause us to fantasize about solving all problems and saving the world. We may be so helpful in the good works that we do not let the others help themselves. These elements are a real part of today's society; however, they do not fit into the self-forgetfulness that is so much a part of the higher mansions, especially the seventh mansion. A true expression of compassionate action is the only way the compassion of Jesus can be extended to others.

Good works, if they are to be deeply connected with Christ, do not flow from being a member of a prestigious organization that does good for some underprivileged group. It is not maintaining our secure positions in life while doling out money to those less fortunate. It is not a feeling sorry for but doing nothing for those people who are caught in the grip of poverty, pain or any other abnormal situation. Christ's compassion involves getting under the skin of those with tears in their eyes and looking out into the world through those eyes. Christ's compassion is being so united with the indwelling presence of God that our outward daily expressions are a reflection of that indwelling. Christ's compassion is not set aside for a specific time and place, but a normal event that is as continuous as a heart beating. Christ's compassion is not ministering to others within a sense of duty, but ministering to others because we truly believe in them, love them, trust them and hope in them. Christ's compassion is not doing things for others, but letting them do things by themselves in their own way so that they may find beauty and strength in their own creations. Through our feeble attempts to extend Christ's compassion to others, we find that we receive more than we give. Christ's compassion can only flow from a grateful heart and the delicate synchronizing of authentic compassionate prayer and authentic compassionate action. When striving for this synchronization, we seldom think of ourselves. Compassion calls us to rise above and go beyond our own desires in prayer and action. Compassion plunges us into the anguish of others so that we may suffer with them and empathetically share in their pain.

Fully alive in Christ

Transformation in God does not mean a loss of our humanness. It means a greater merging of our humanness within the humanity of Jesus. Through Jesus we become fully human and fully alive.

Now, by becoming more human within the humanity of Jesus, we do not strive to become better than human. To reach for anything beyond what Jesus has given us through his humanity is to be spiritually disoriented. To avoid spiritual disorientation, we keep away from a tendency to speak without humor or feeling, a task-oriented approach to all areas of life and a preoccupation with compulsive activities, intellectual pursuits, or projects to accomplish. Spiritual orientation is to be aware of our own playful intuition, personal identity, quixotic insights, fanciful creativity, magical poetic abilities and the wonder, beauty, and power of our sexuality. We wholeheartedly grasp the message of the incarnate Christ. In the spirit of Jesus, wholeness is not out of balance. It is an ongoing, creative integration of all elements of our humanity which are bonded together by a dynamic spirituality.

To be fully human is to journey within a process in which we become more integrated through a healthy blending of holiness and wholeness. Through this process we come to terms with and accept the light and dark forces in our personality. We are open to God speaking to us through all the experiences in our lives. His still, small voice comes through the external world outside and the internal world within. This often transcends the happiness of the now and replaces it with the pain that comes through change and growth. Thomas Merton illustrates the blending of holiness and wholeness when he said, "Sanctity is not a matter of being less human but more human. It is a greater capacity for concern, for suffering, for understanding, for sympathy and for humor, for joy and for the appreciation of the good and beautiful things in life." Jesus shows that to be truly holy and wholesome we must have a great capacity to love. He showed the greatness of this love when he gave his life. Love requires courage in order for it to be authentic. Love comes from wounded, gentle pilgrims who have dared to step out of the lines of conformity and run risks as Jesus did.

What are some of the personal characteristics that may develop in the seventh mansion? It might be well to reflect upon some of the traits that spring from the personality of the one who presented the concept of the interior castle. Teresa had a tendency to be tenacious and hardheaded when faced with solving the problems of her day. She was not awed by power or prestige shown by those outside of or in the Church. Her manner was oftentimes blunt when she desired to right the wrongs that she saw. Despite trouble, apathy, aggression and wearisome trials, she refused to lose heart. Surrounding everything was Teresa's ever present, sometimes caustic, sense of humor. This got her through the bad patches and rough terrain of her life's journey. Laughter has also become the sun that warms our pilgrims on their damp and dismal days in life.

The deep contentment that flows from the seventh mansion gives our pilgrim a quietness within any desire to find happiness in another environment. The grass is always greener on the other side of the fence mentality has once and for all been laid aside. Our pilgrim knows that many places or life styles look good from the road, but no place or life style is without problems. It was learned several mansions ago that there was no such thing as the perfect spouse, child, community, parent, superior, supervisor or environment. This deep contentment also remains when our pilgrim feels out of sorts for one reason or another, or feels that he or she is in the lower levels of wellness or integration. There is a mellow rootedness in being where one now is. Our pilgrim is living fully in the present with a jovial enthusiasm and a great capacity for work. He or she experiences a deep gratitude for all that has been and all that is and will be.

A continual growing into the infinite Christ is made through accepting the vitality of all the areas of one's being, through the harmonizing of a balanced, flexible and spiritualized personality and through acknowledging faults, foibles, and failures. All is given to Jesus and our pilgrim finds his or her authentic and unique self through him, in him and with him. An individual has learned to live in compassion with self and with others. All are now bonded together by imperfections and weaknesses, yet the pilgrim experiences a freedom, a suppleness, and a vulnerability that recaptures the vision of a child. One is brought back to a time that was present before selfishness. A great simplicity turns speech about God into a song. There is resting of the Beloved in the beloved, being one with the One and growing deeply in the wholeness of the love from this being. Our pilgrim's gaze is fixed on Jesus. He is both companion and goal. The fire of this gaze burns from the simplicity of being transparent before him. A desire to enkindle the healing warmth of God's love in every person whose life our pilgrim touches is perpetually present.

The intense intimacy with God has expanded one's humanness to its greatest potential. A pilgrim is living from the inside out. He or she is spontaneous, warm, available, approachable, down to earth and practical. A new dawn has transformed every action and duty of the day to a yes to God. There is a continual searching and seeking to do what he is asking at every moment. In whatever life style a person is living, he or she has learned that each moment is lived in love and trust. A bonding in love and trust nurtures one's life in God and God's life within.

In the seventh mansion all aspects of our pilgrim's life converge into a perpetual praise. There is the internal loving communion with God and the external flow of service to others. All reflect a sound and tender love for the gentle Jesus. The profundity of what has happened in this mansion is held in the secret places of the heart. Our pilgrim's thoughts turn once again to Mary who pondered deeply and lovingly within her heart. She treasured the events that led to the birth of her Son. She did not speak much about them, nor did she speak much about Jesus' growth during his boyhood years. These were intimate times shared only with Joseph. Their combined song of praise was constant and quiet, rising to God as smoke from burning incense ascends from a thurible.

Our service to others, too, are secret gifts that give simple praise to God. They are given quietly and without flourish. Involuntary suffering, extra time spent in prayer, not complaining when a rainstorm cancels a picnic, or not showing impatience when listening to a story that we have heard ten times before from the same person are inconspicuous gifts to God when given in a low key manner. Simple gifts are given quite naturally. We may volunteer to drive someone to the doctor's, to a meeting, or to a leisure time activity without having the person ask for a ride. We may clean up a messy kitchen or cook a meal without having the need called to our attention. We remain calm when irritated by answering the doorbell and telephone which ring very often and both at the same time. These all indicate that we are able to live the life of simple gifts freely given.

In the seventh mansion with the loved friend, transparency to the other is a person's only desire. There is total self-forgetfulness here. There is no longer a fear of the pain that is involved in loving. Together with the other there is a heart union that is deeply bonded in the continual dying and rising that comes along the road of life. Many facets about the shared life with the other are held more secretly than before. The love within this relationship continues to require self-disclosure, and the depths of what is given to the other is for the other alone. This goes far beyond mere confidentiality. These intimate sharings are treasured and buried in the recesses of the heart. Many nonverbal sharings are so precious that words would only spoil them. The creative power of God's love is expressed in its fullest measure between heart friend and heart friend. Each joyfully radiates the peace of Christ. There are no labels or roles for the heart friends for they were dropped some time ago, nor are there images or symbols of the God within. Here an individual authentically and sincerely knows the deep riches that flow from an intimate friendship with Christ. The friendship of Christ is reflected ever so beautifully from the heart of one's dearly beloved friend.

Our pilgrims have learned that the deep love experienced in a relationship with a beloved friend has groomed and prepared them for the depths of God's love. The intimacy, tenderness, and compassion that was found as this union grew has taught our pilgrims about the intimacy, tenderness, and compassion of God. Within the higher mansions the heart friends have brought the beauty in each other to full fruition. The friends are now knit together in a special covenant of love which is rooted in grace, honesty, acceptance, forgiveness, pain and a translucence whereby the loved other knows the beloved better than the beloved knows himself or herself. The heart friends' spiritual lives have matured and have become well integrated into their personhood. All developmental areas have been uplifted through God's graces and the interaction and experience of human and divine love. The special faith and special love the beloved friends have learned to share now bonds them soundly and securely in each other and in God. After the third mansion, sacrifice was found necessary to sustain this type of friendship. Somewhere within the higher mansions each has offered his or her life to God as a sacrifice for the growth, in Christ, of the loved other. This mutual sacrifice was a loving oblation which brought two together as one in a mutual self-giving to God. A loving oblation united two as one in love. The love, then, overflows and is shared with all humankind. Love has transformed two persons forever into one spirit. The two hearts that were joined as one heart in the fifth mansion will be eternally as one, and this heart is beating boldly, bravely, consistently, and lovingly in the great heart of Christ.

POSTLUDE

This brings us to the end of our journey through the seven mansions. The harmonic blending of these mansions has ended. Teresa's symphony of love is now complete. Her exquisite melodies have all been sung. Their beauty will echo forever down the centuries.

This journey is open to all who have a great thirst for God and a sincere love for his Son. A person need not be a member of the clergy or a religious to make the journey, nor does an individual need an affiliation with the Carmelite order.

It has been said that a pilgrimage through the interior castle is only one path among the many paths that lead to God. It also has been said that extraordinary events within a person's spiritual life are the exception rather than the rule. During her years in Carmel, Therese of Lisieux walked a path that was totally barren of extraordinary mystical experiences. She lived at a time when extraordinary favors were a sure indication of authentic spirituality. This did not dampen her own perspective on holiness. Perfectly content with her "little way" she journeyed onward in Carmel. During the last year and a half of her life Therese underwent a dark night of the soul. This was a blood and guts experience for her. Steps along this road were initiated only by her strong courage and her ever burning faith. She traveled bravely through her dark night. As always, she made the best of it. She saw Jesus present in her darkness.

So it is not where we are, but where we are going that matters. When considering the hills and valleys of our own spiritual journey, it is wise to keep these often quoted words of Teresa in mind:

> Let nothing disturb you.
> Let nothing frighten you.
> For all things pass save God
> Who does not change.
> Be patient, and at the last
> You will find
> All fulfillment.
> Hold God, and nothing
> Will fail you.
> For he alone is all.

BIBLIOGRAPHY

Abbott, Walter M., ed. *The Documents of Vatican II*. Piscataway: New Century Publishing, Inc., 1966.

Aumann, Jordan. *Teresa's Interior Castle*, Modern Cassette Library. Notre Dame: Ave Maria Press.

Boersig, Teresa. "The Seven Mansions: Prayer and Relationship" in *Review for Religious* 40/1 (January-February 1981).

Burrows, Ruth. *Fire Upon the Earth: Interior Castle Explored*. Denville: Dimension Books, 1981.

Cannan, Noreen. "Becoming Holy and Whole," in *Human Development* 3/1 (Spring 1982).

de la Vega, Carmen Mary. "The Prayer of Quiet," in *Spiritual Life* 24/2 (Summer 1978).

Foster, Richard J. *Celebration of Discipline: The Path to Spiritual Growth*. San Francisco: Harper and Row, 1978.

Groeschel, Benedict J. *Listening at Prayer*. Ramsey: Paulist Press, 1984.

Hammett, Rosine, Sofield, Loughlan. *Inside Christian Community*. Jesuit Educational Center for Human Development. Le Jaq Publishing, Inc., 1974.

Hinnebusch, Paul. *Friendship in the Lord*. Notre Dame: Ave Maria Press, 1974.

Huss, A. Joy. "Touch With Care or a Caring Touch?" 1976 Eleanor Clarke Slagle Lecture, Annual Conference of the American Occupational Therapy Association. *American Journal of Occupational Therapy* 31/1 (January 1977).

Malarkey, Lucy, and Dorothy Marron. "Evaluating Community Interaction," in *Human Development* 3/3 (Fall 1982).

Mary of Jesus and St. Joseph. *Friendship With Christ: Love and Service*. Schenectady: Carmel, 1972.

Morrison, Douglas, Donald McNeill, and Henri Nouwen. *Compassion: A Reflection on the Christian Life*. New York: Doubleday, 1982.

McNamara, William. *Mystical Passion: Spirituality for a Bored Society*. Ramsey: Paulist Press, 1977.

Peck, M. Scott. *The Road Less Traveled: A New Psychology of Love, Traditional Values, and Spiritual Growth*. New York: Simon and Schuster, 1978.

Samuels, Mike, and Hal Bennett. *The Well Body Book.* New York: Random House, 1973.

Seeliger, Wes. "Western Theology," in *Desert Call* 16/1 (Spring 1981).

Teresa of Avila, Saint. *The Collected Works of St. Teresa of Avila,* vol. 2, transl. by Otilio Rodriguez and Kieran Kavanaugh. Washington, D.C.: ICS Publications, 1980.